BETWEEN SOVEREIGNTY AND INTEGRATION

GOVERNMENT AND OPPOSITION

A quarterly journal of comparative politics, published by Government and Opposition, with the assistance of the London School of Economics and Political Science, Houghton Street, London, WC2A 2AE

BETWEEN SOVEREIGNTY AND INTEGRATION

edited by

GHITA IONESCU

A HALSTED PRESS BOOK

JOHN WILEY & SONS
New York—Toronto

© GOVERNMENT AND OPPOSITION LTD.

PUBLISHED IN THE U.S.A., CANADA AND
LATIN AMERICA BY HALSTED PRESS,
A DIVISION OF JOHN WILEY AND SONS INC.,
NEW YORK

ISBN: 0-470-42800-7

LIBRARY OF CONGRESS CATALOG CARD NUMBER: 73-19586

PRINTED IN GREAT BRITAIN

Contents

Ghiţa Ionescu

Between Sovereignty and Integration: Introduction

WHEN KARL DEUTSCH STARTED TO PREPARE THE 'SECOND THEME' OF
the IXth World Congress of the International Political Science
Association held in Montreal in August 1973, entitled *'Key Issues in
International Conflict and Peace Research'* he asked me to organize the
Commission which was to deal with the problem: *Pathways to Peace:
National Sovereignty or Supranational Integration.*

The task of trying to disentangle all the questions linked in this
rather formidable subject seemed to me to require first of all a working definition of its various aspects, then a great number of papers* to
examine at least those aspects which I considered essential in the
light of the working definition; and a good discussion to wrap them
together again. I tried to propose the working definition. The nine
contributions here published are the actual papers which were discussed at Montreal. And the discussion seemed to achieve, with
less difficulty than was feared, an ultimate coherence, expressed
with his usual vigour by Karl Deutsch in his concluding remarks
also published here.

---

* The nine papers, in alphabetic order of the contributors, were as follows:
David E. Apter, 'The Premise of Parliamentary Planning'; Max Beloff, 'The
Political Crisis of the European Nation-States'; David Coombes, '"Concertation"
in the Nation-State and in the European Community'; Leon Dion, 'Anti-
Politics and Marginals'; Geoffrey Goodwin, 'The Erosion of External
Sovereignty'; 'Luxemburgensis', 'The Emergence of a European Sovereignty';
Dennis Kavanagh, 'Beyond Autonomy? The Politics of Corporations'; Donald
J. Puchala, 'Internal Order and Peace: an Integrated Europe in World Affairs'
and Herbert J. Spiro, 'Interdependence: A Third Option Between National
Sovereignty and Supranational Integration'. Two further papers by Karl
Pomaizl (Prague) and Ioan Ceterchi (Bucharest) were circulated at Montreal by
the authors themselves, and were included in the panel discussion as auxiliary
reports.

The role assigned to the commission was to discuss the question posed in its title: *Pathways to Peace: National Sovereignty or Supranational Integration?* (Interrogation mark added.) In longhand, and in contemporary terms, the question could read thus. 'What is more likely to lead to peace (or conversely to war) in the industrial, or post-industrial age: The new politics, say of *balkanization*, i.e. the erratic behaviour of a multitude of precarious nation-states perhaps no longer capable of mastering their own fates and prone to produce internal and external crises, or the new politics of, say, *balance of power*, in which modern federations, integrating vast and viable territorial units, would zone the world under their influence?'

The argument thus formulated both links and opposes, at three centuries distance and with entirely different socio-economic backgrounds, the classic theory of sovereignty as proposed by Hobbes, and the modern theory of integration, as proposed by Karl Deutsch and others. What do these theories have in common?

First, their attitudes towards peace are normative. For Hobbes, war was the worst evil. 'The final cause, and or design of men is the foresight of getting themselves out of that miserable condition of war.' Whereas Aristotle or Machiavelli were distinctly ambivalent on the subject of the alternation of the two, to them, natural conditions.

Admittedly Hobbes was speaking under the immediate impact of civil war. But he abhorred strife in itself and feared its spreading disorder, its inevitable escalation. He believed that any kind of disorder could lead to further involvements once it raged somewhere. Here then is the second Hobbes-like approach of this discussion: in the linkage it operates between internal order-versus-disorder and external order-versus-disorder.

But the notion of national sovereignty is not opposed in the logic of this argument to the notion of integration. This would be a *non-sequitur* because ultimately the two notions seen from this point of view are almost tautological. Their common ultimate purpose is to achieve cohesion, order and stability, indeed to fulfil Hobbes's quest for the institutionalization of the 'Commonwealth' (today an ambivalent expression).

But then when seen together in that particular moment of history when the condition of the industrial society reveals the need for other kinds of government, other styles of politics than those which the liberal, laissez-faire, nation-state can offer,[1] the two notions differ in two ways.

The first is the difference in the level at which each can be effective i.e. at which level can political cohesion, order and stability best be achieved in the industrial age: at the national or at the supranational level? From this point of view the question we were asked seemed to me to be actually two questions. The first runs as follows: if national sovereignties were to be further eroded, will there be another possibility of reconstructing the political stability, which has been weakened within the nation-states, at a higher, supranational level? And the second: if order at the level of the nation-state can no longer be made to prevail (Hobbes's 'kingdom divided in itself cannot stand'), will the disorder also invade the international level in an escalation: internal strife – civil-war – war? Thus, whichever way we look at it, the fundamental question to be discussed here by students of politics, as distinct from students of international relations, is how can political coherence, order and stability prevail both internally and externally in the post-industrial society?

The other difference lies in the political processes with which sovereignty and integration are respectively credited. Sovereignty is seen as the articulation of the relations of power-obedience, protection-allegiance, between the 'strong central power' and its subjects through the mechanisms of representation, accountability, and coercion. Integration is a process of interpenetration of different degrees of autonomy and, to quote Deutsch again, 'is formed by a multiplicity of ranges of social communication'.

THE TWO SETS OF OPTIONS OF GOVERNABILITY

I was naturally interested in attempting to answer Karl Deutsch's question, because I happen to have worked for some years on a book 'on the governability of industrial societies, with special

---

[1] 'The issue of political integration thus arose primarily when people demanded greater capabilities, greater performance, greater responsiveness and more adequate services from the governments of the political units by which they had been governed before', Karl Deutsch, ed., in *Political Community and the North Atlantic Area – International Organization in the Light of Experience*, Princeton, 1957, p. 87.

regard to Europe' to be published this year. Although the book examines the problem with a different purpose, nevertheless it does deal explicitly with the *national* side, and implicitly, but logically inevitably, with the *international* side, of Karl Deutsch's dialectic question.

The theme of the book is that the highly industrialized societies of the technological age, and more particularly those of Western Europe, are faced with two sets of options in the search for a solution to the problem of what is called here governability. The first is the choice between national and supranational government. The second choice is that between representative government and direct administration.

But two preliminary observations must be made here. One is that though these two sets of choices may present themselves at the same time, they do not necessarily do so, they are not indissolubly linked, logically, or historically. Adopting a particular alternative from the first pair of options does not necessarily affect the choice that will be made between the second pair. Happy economic results of federalization might predispose a state differently towards the re-structuration of its social and political institutions. Alternatively, intensive pressure for social and political change in a given state might lead to the postponement or complete abandonment of that state's initial project to integrate with others. Moreover, social and international problems do not always arise together nor can they be jointly solved. States which are already federated, for instance, are nevertheless beset with socio-economic problems.

Secondly, it must be observed that if the alternative national/supranational government has now become a familiar expression, the second alternative, representative government/direct administration is put forward here in terms much more trenchant, in a more dramatic contrast, than in the usual public formulations. In industrial communist societies – which, in their own constitutional theory, are meant to operate the transition towards direct administration – discussion of this particular alternative approach to government is silenced by means of political control. In capitalist societies, the issue has not yet crystallized so clearly as to justify the blunt terms in which the contrast is stated here. But this formulation has been deliberately chosen in order to pin-point the crux of the social and political crisis of all highly industrial societies. One should however constantly keep in mind that political practice and political reality always blurr and distort the hypotheses of political theory. Moreover, political theories which favour one system of government as against another often concur in the belief that in logic, as in ultimate reality, systems complement each other. The two spokesmen for the systems contrasted here, J. B. Mill, and Saint Simon, prove the point. For Mill, participation by the citizens in administration was the necessary ingredient of representative government; for Saint Simon, electoral representation was an essential mechanism of direct administration.

Turning to the option national/supranational government, nine Western European states have now officially proclaimed their decision to work in common towards their integration. If this enterprise is carried to a successful conclusion, the union of the nine states will, it is estimated, be as well equipped to survive and prosper in the technological age as the existing federations – the USA and the USSR – have proved to be. But the enterprise is still under way and subject to much controversy. Hence the dramatic character of this course of action for Western Europe. Eastern Europe too is officially committed to further measures of integration. But national and international conditions differ so much between the two regions of Europe, that one can only conclude that 'integration' means something different in the two contexts.

In the second set of choices, representative government or direct administration, a word must be said about the latter. Self-management, to give direct administration a name by which it is also known, is now demanded by, or on behalf of, the 'producers', or 'the corporate forces' of the highly industrial societies. The increasingly successful attempts of these forces to emancipate themselves from the tutelage of governments claiming to represent the entire national community, and from the tutelage of other representative institutions such as the political parties and where applicable, parliaments, have affected all the states and the political systems of industrial societies. It was not sheer coincidence which led two highly industrial European states, one, capitalist, France, the other, communist, Czechoslovakia, to undergo simultaneously the most shattering political crises, in spring 1968, arising in both cases from the demand for 'participation'.

The question posed here is whether the West European societies which have until now been organized as nation-states and have been governed by the complex of representative institutions which together form representative government or modern political sovereignty, will continue to be governable in the technological age in the same way and by the same means? Or will they be subjected from within to increasing tensions arising from confrontations between their component groups which might in time lead to 'internal war', to use Harry Eckstein's expression, if not civil war; and from without to increasing stresses on their own power of decision-making, thus rendering the function of the sovereign, 'to maintain order in my territory against threats from within and from without' increasingly illusory? Ungovernability, thus, in the context of the highly industrial societies, must be taken to mean the dissolution of the bonds of allegiance and the failure of the rule of law within a sovereign nation-state, in which sovereignty has been based, since the 19th century at least, on the complex of institutions representing the will of the people. Meanwhile, these same societies, in the earnest search for governability, engender, under our eyes, new forms of political organization: mixed national and supranational, and mixed representative and corporate social and political institutions.

CASES AND SITUATIONS

Here are cases and situations which can illustrate the main aspects of the problem. Take for instance Italy for a scenario. Italy is a state beset by all the centrifugal stresses of a modern society: economic (its large industrial corporations are unaccountable to the state, and the level of development between the north and the south is most uneven), social (its trade unions are politically emancipated and there is permanent industrial unrest), regional (its autonomous regions recognize only with difficulty the authority of the central government, but expect it to subsidize them) and last but not least political (there is an anti-system opposition representing between a quarter to a third of the population) as well as by strong religious and ideological problems. Leaders in the Italian national press constantly give to more impressionable readers the feeling that a collapse of the entire 'system' might be imminent. Now, *suppose* that this did happen, even now when the new detente in East–West relations renders such dramatic developments less likely than they were say, three years ago: would the Italian crisis be contained to a national drama, or would it soon produce a major international confrontation? And vice versa, *suppose* that Italy had not been a member of the European community and thus, albeit loosely, integrated within a community of states directly interested in ensuring that a modicum of economic prosperity, of social peace, of political order and of international security should be ensured to this admirable country beset with problems – would these problems, already so difficult to solve, not have been even more acute for an isolated Italy?

Or take the case of Britain. When the British government presided over by Mr Wilson, applied in 1969 for admission to the European Economic Community and therefore made an explicit pledge gradually to renounce some of the elements of its national sovereignty and to engage in a long-term operation of European integration, Britain as a nation-state, was faced with grave problems of governability. Centrifugal trends had set in which were rendering steering from the centre increasingly difficult. Thus, the pound sterling, the monetary symbol of national sovereignty, was frequently exposed to the crisis raging in the monetary system of the free world. Then in Northern Ireland, a region of the United Kingdom which was particularly sensitive to religious, national and social conflicts, sovereignty was to be twice challenged: first the sovereignty of Ulster located in Stormont was suspended and replaced by direct rule from Westminster; and then British military rule was itself doubly challenged, both by the Irish Catholic and by the Protestant population of Ulster.[2] Thirdly, and perhaps most important of all, the British economy as a whole was being increasingly hampered by social conflicts. This, of course, was a general feature of all industrial societies, and especially of the West European ones. But in Britain it was aggravated, among other things, also by a lack of organization in industrial relations which compared unfavourably with the organization of industrial relations in, for instance, the United States, the Federal Republic of Germany or Sweden. It was in such negative conditions, and preoccupied with such signs of national disarray that the British government, under Mr Wilson, sought to explore the prospects of supranational integration.

Obviously what the British pro-marketeers hoped to find in this extraordinary (in the sense of extra-national as well as unprecedented) departure, was not a direct and immediate answer to crises like the three which have been singled out. What they sought was,

[2] The recently published *Report of the Royal Commission on the Constitution* (HMSO, Cmnd 5460, 1973) amounts in effect to a re-examination of the condition of the sovereignty of the United Kingdom after the more recent national and international events which have affected it.

on the contrary, a larger framework and a long-term perspective from which such national crises could be cut down to size, and from which the real causes of constant deterioration could be properly assessed and tackled. British policy-making had been confined since the end of the second world war, since decolonization and since the coming of high technology, in the vicious circle of steady economic deterioration. For although the British welfare state proved to be a most positive answer to the question of how to reconcile the quest for increased social justice with the quest for increased political participation (which, in turn, are the pre-requisites of the functioning of a modern industrial society), the British economy since the inauguration of the welfare state has shown a constant downward trend. Within the league of European economies the British economy gradually dropped from the top to the bottom. Socialist and conservative governments, alternating in power, had shown themselves equally unsuccessful in arresting this decline.

It is at this logical junction that the chronic British economic problem revealed its political implications and actuality. Public opinion, seeing that these alternating governments were equally impotent, in spite of their different approaches and of their different ideologies, to solve the principal economic problems, began to doubt that they could ever find, within the present conditions, the proper remedy. Government itself, or indeed the representative government of the British nation-state, was losing its credibility. This deep crisis of confidence came more clearly into the open in the 1960s, or what is usually called the post-Suez era. A mood of impatience overtook the mature and patient British public opinion. Unsuccessful regimes, however admirable their intentions or difficult their problems, are always in history held responsible by weary peoples. Some of the British people and especially the industrial workers led, in the post-Suez era, by a new generation of militant shop-stewards and/or trade union leaders, some of whom in any case preferred corporate rule to parliamentary government for ideological reasons, drew with gusto on the poor record of the 'system' as a whole. Other elements of British public opinion believed that the poor performance of the British economy was due to the inherent insufficiency of the economic basis of the post-colonial British nation-state. After all the two super-powers of the technological age are both federations, commanding vast territorial mainlands and enormous pools of economic resources. And, at Britain's very doorstep, the first decade of the European economic integration (1957–1967) created earlier by

European powers aware of the basic insufficiencies of their individual national economies, had proved to be a distinct success, not only for the community as a whole, but for the economy of each individual member-state of this community of democracies. This realization helped to make Britain engage in the experiments of supranational integration.

But at the same time 'the European Economic Community was seen by its founders as the thin economic end of a thick political wedge . . . in the minds of the draftsmen of the Treaty, the gradual process of practical economic integration was intended to lead to eventual political union or integration' as Lord Crowther-Hunt and Professor A. T. Peacock remind us in their timely re-examination of the British constitution since the entry of Britain in the EEC.[3] The political purpose preceded and comprehended the economic finality.

But the way in which the European Community was formed, and in particular the common traits of the states which compose it, warrant two more general remarks which, even if well known, are relevant to the question discussed. It is relevant to remember in this context that the homogeneity of size and status of the would-be partners was a factor which facilitated, indeed justified, their mutual decision to integrate. There was no super-power amongst them which, by the very disequilibrium which it would create in the integrative relations, would have made them cling to their 'sovereignty' rather than engage in an operation inevitably leading to outright domination by an overpowering confederate. To be sure, the member states of the EEC are watching each other's moves and intentions with obvious intensity in the constant 'bargaining' which is the policy-making of the Council of Ministers. But this is rather the proof that they can oppose and resist the designs of domination of any of the partners. In the case of the formation of the EEC, the previous assessment by the future members of the chances and risks of sovereignty and integration respectively, weighed in favour of the latter.

It is also relevant to recall here that in the case of the members of the European Economic Communities, all of them constitutional pluralistic states, with increasingly active public opinions, the possibility of having to share the external sovereignty of the state with

[3] Lord Crowther-Hunt and Professor A. T. Peacock: *Memorandum of Dissent*, volume II of Report of the Royal Commission on the Constitution, p. 37.

other states, was preceded by the realization that, internally, the state, or the central government, had been sharing its 'sovereignty' increasingly with other forces in the society. The act of sharing, or to put it in another way, the quest for integration, was effected simultaneously in the two inseparably dialectic aspects of 'sovereignty'. Integration in the internal policy-making processes should thus facilitate supranational integration, in the case of states reasonably equal in territorial size, economic resources and international status—and vice versa.

The final example can be drawn from the theories put forward in the Montreal discussion in the auxiliary reports originating from Czechoslovakia and Romania (and included in the forthcoming volume in the chapter 'Two Views from Eastern Europe').[4] These theories might be considered also as a litmus-paper test of some of the general remarks made here on the subject of the European Economic Community.

The two reports, although they differ on the issue of the survival of the nation, stress that the present regional co-ordination in Eastern Europe should be seen for the time being at least, not as supranational integration but only as free co-operation between sovereign states, with the accent still laid on the sovereignty and the independence of each of the partners. This is the official attitude of most governments participating in the regional organization of the Council for Political and Economic Assistance and especially of the government of the Romanian Socialist Republic. What mattered more for the discussion in Montreal was the logical nexus which this attitude operated (and which is clearly articulated in Professor Ceterchi's report) between the full *control* by the *state* of its external policy, as well as of all the internal policies: social, economic, industrial, educational, and otherwise. This confirmed once more that there were different alternatives of governability according on the one hand, to the type of political regime: highly centralized political regimes which rely even in the industrial-technological age on the direct and total controls of the sovereign state, or constitutional pluralistic regimes which accept increasingly the realities of the diffusion of internal and external sovereignty; and, on the other hand, different alternatives of integration according to the size and status

---

[4] See below, pp. 135–42. 'Two Views from Eastern Europe' based on the reports presented by Professor Karel Pomaizl, from Prague, and Professor I. Ceterchi, from Bucharest.

of the different states, small, medium, or super-powers, and the relative degree of 'interdependence' of the would-be partners.

THE DISCUSSION

Although fully aware of the ultimate limitations of a 'panel' coping with such an encyclopaedic range of questions, we tried to organize the argument in, as it were, stages of its own unfolding, going from the aspects of the governability of sovereign nation-states to those of the effects which regional integration might have on peace.

This logical order of ideas starts with Max Beloff's concise but sharp analysis of the change of status and of scope of the post-colonial European powers, and of the economic, social and political consequences of this reduction to their metropolitan sizes and resources.

The discussion continues then with Léon Dion's dramatic case-study of Quebec – a double case-study in effect as it presents the problem of the centrifugal and violent 'groups' in the industrial society, and that of the increased difficulties in collaboration between regions in all contemporary states, but of necessity even more so in the federal communities of the technological age. Léon Dion's handling of this pivotal stage in the argument is conceptual in so far as it discusses the problem of violent disruption in all industrial societies in general (say in France in 1968 or in Northern Ireland now) but it develops the argument up to the possibility of civil war, and therefore takes the academic discussions into the reality of the most dreaded perspectives of the end of sovereignty.

Dennis Kavanagh discusses the multinational corporations and their effect on the sovereignty of nation-states. This is of course a subject which has attracted, and still attracts a lot of authors, journalists, reporters, essayists, situated at the borders of political science, and thus free to 'sensationalize' the subject and to over-dramatize it to the liking of populist and radical readers. Dennis Kavanagh, on the contrary, takes a low-key approach; circumscribes as much as required the problem to what it should be in reality, and while not concluding that the 'monsters' or the 'juggernauts' are there in the dark shadow of our society ready to swallow our sovereignties and our freedoms, concludes that generally speaking multinational corporations raise serious problems of accountability in the nation-state. Moreover, what I find particularly relevant in Kavanagh's approach is the way in which it seems to accept as a

fait accompli of contemporary political thinking what he defines as
'the transnational penetration and reaction which link the national
and international political systems' and 'the interface of government
and corporation, crossing the boundaries of politics and economics'.
These definitions might sound platitudinous, and some readers might
wonder why such obvious truisms, so frequently repeated, should be
singled out here. The point is, however, that many readers may not
be readily aware of the gulf which separates the public formulation
of such views, and the mental readiness of political practitioners and
public alike to *accept* these views, let alone to use them as the basic
groundwork for their analysis and method of assessment. Old
prejudices, like old soldiers are hard to kill.

This digression, with its homiletic overtones, occurred as I was
reaching, in the recapitulation of our discussions, the point where,
leaving behind the critical analysis of the governability of the nation-
state, we started on the uphill road to the problem of the feasibility
of integration in Western Europe and of the effect this would have
on the peace of the world. Here the fluctuating borderline between
the *positive* and the *imaginative* approaches was fascinating to follow,
especially perhaps to Karl Deutsch and myself, who had been
responsible for posing the – perhaps unanswerable – questions.

Take, for instance David Apter's paper, 'The Premise of Parliamentary Planning'.[5] His idea of uniting two institutions, which by
their very nature and method of functioning are opposed to each
other, Parliament and Plan, inevitably seems Utopian to positive
analysts of contemporary society. Planning need not of course
always be the quintessence of central controls which it is in the
USSR, where it was also meant to serve a dictatorial regime. But even
when planning exists in the mildest of consultative forms, as for
instance it did, and still does to a certain extent, in the Fifth French
Republic, it is bound to encroach on parliamentary sovereignty and
to reduce the role of parliament, in so far as the latter is called upon
only at the end of the 'consultations' to choose between major
options and, ultimately, to endorse somewhat blindly the result of
the consultations. And, vice-versa, parliaments themselves are
obviously handicapped by their functional inability and lack of
competence to cope with the sheer volume and mass of detail com-
prised in a long term plan, and to provide the a-political expertise
required by long term planning. Yet there is no way out – if the
future society is to avoid the excesses of bureaucratic centralism of

[5] First published in *Government and Opposition*, *op. cit.*

the contemporary planning states, and the economic fortuity of the contemporary non-planning states. Parliament is the only institution able to represent the community freely as a whole. Can it not adapt itself to the need of the modern communities for economic concert? Moreover communities themselves are changing. In Western Europe, national political communities which have come to the bitter realization that their national resources, political and economic, are insufficient, are striving to join forces in a supranational community. They naturally feel the need for a supranational European Parliament. Here the institution imagined by David Apter, in another context, might come in. The institutionalization of the new Parliament (which will inevitably be formed if the EEC survives) should profit from the lessons of the past and reject the old arbitrary distinctions between national and international, representative and corporate, political and economic. The European Parliament should be a new body which would, by its very structure, combine these previously disparate, hostile and blinkered interests into one, major, deliberative body. How Utopian must this seem to those who consider even the present transnational debates and exchanges of the European Parliament too far removed from the safe base of national politics!

Or take for instance the engaging trio of concepts defended in their papers by Goodwin, Luxemburgensis, Puchala, and Spiro: sovereignty, integration and interdependence respectively. The four papers reflect an objective and modern approach by proposing a critical analysis of each of these concepts. Goodwin underlines the need to redefine sovereignty and to accommodate it to the requirements of the modern international world. But he shrewdly draws attention to the effect which integrative policies may have (and indeed have had) on national communities, namely to lead to a heightened consciousness and pursuit of the national interest within the supranational sphere. In his paper on 'The Emergence of a European Sovereignty' Luxemburgensis describes the gradual transition of some attributes of sovereignty to the community.

Spiro takes us straight to the *Realpolitik* of the diplomacy of the 1970s. He sees it as conditioned by the interdependence of the world as a whole, and more particularly by the interdependent pentagon of powers. Hence his insistence that 'the influence of sovereignty, integration and associated concepts has been so pervasive . . . that I almost feel we need to lift ourselves up by our conceptual bootstraps in order to view this history as the expansion of consciousness of interdependence'. He then proceeds with the critical analysis of the concept of interdependence which he had put forward.

Puchala deals with the concept of integration. Puchala's study provides historical depth by giving us a comparative analysis of the behaviour of units which have 'integrated' in the past, before the present experiment was launched. Such an analysis can help to predict the ways in which the EEC (should it ever be completed) might behave in the international arena. In a sober final assessment, he puts forward the view that if the EEC does not falter through faults of leadership and structure, it might presently enter into what he describes as the 'assertive' phase in the evolution of newly integrated communities before they mature into constructive participants in an adjusted international system.

In his conclusion, Deutsch brings us back to the central problem. Having heard Beloff, Dion, Kavanagh and Apter on the subject of the inadequacy of the present institutions of the nation-state for coping with the stresses and strains put upon them by the social and economic developments of the technological age; and having heard the analyses by Goodwin, Spiro and Puchala of the viability of three concepts, sovereignty, integration and interdependence, in the context of the present international crisis, Deutsch, in the end draws our attention to *integration* and also to *concertation* as more useful concepts. It is therefore to his definition of integration that we must refer, and I cannot resist quoting from his concluding text which seems to me to give coherence to the entire discussion: 'Integration' says Deutsch, 'even of the pluralistic kind, requires a very high degree of integration of the social fabric' . . . and further, 'We can no longer drive any substantial minority, or any major ethnic or social group, to desperation'; and finally 'dependable [international] co-ordination cannot be built by deterrence and bargaining alone. A world of deterrent powers, a world of bargaining powers will, as a total system, be ungovernable. There will be no invisible hand to keep the system together, or to move it anywhere.' Deutsch's interpretation of the theory of integration shows its relevance in the West European context. It might well be that a single 'model' will fail to materialize. The comparative schemes of 'integration' in Latin America, Eastern Europe, the Middle East and Western Europe were too dissimilar, or especially too inconclusive, to enable a pattern to emerge. But the relevance of the concept for the highly industrialized Western European societies was, by the same token, accentuated. For here it was the societies which, less dependent on the states, were adapting themselves to the *Deus-ex-machina* requirements of the technological revolution, of the international economy, of social interpenetration and of mass-communication.

With this, we come to the 'politics of concertation'. David Coombes has contributed a scholarly analysis of this fashionable expression. It is used nowadays especially in French dirigist language and in the language of the European Community to describe the inter-governmental transnational procedure of policy-making of the Council of Ministers.[6] But as it is used more and more frequently so the expression acquires, by extrapolation, or as it were by decantation, a more general meaning. As it is used in the Communitarian vernacular, the phrase 'the politics of concertation' seemed to us to have acquired a new, more abstract sense, which could be amplified in the following terms.

The politics of concertation is the range of actions by which modern public organizations endeavour to feed into their processes of decision-making an adequate amount of information from, and participation by, the socio-economic interests. The public organizations which practise the politics of concertation include national bodies, national governments and international or supranational organizations. The organizations may have a political or an economic focus and they may be geared to systems of either public or private ownership. As is the case with indicative planning (the expression comes from the French *economie concertée* which was one of the ways in which the founders of the French plan described their system), the purpose of concertation is to co-ordinate over a long period of years the socio-economic activities of a community and to direct them towards anticipated targets. Like the politics of collectivism (S. Beer), of corporate pluralism (Rokkan), of consultation (Dion), or of bargaining (Dahl), the politics of concertation

[6] The words *se concerter* and *concertation* in French have the literal meaning of solving questions or preparing actions by mutual consultation. They also have the more distant meaning of 'harmonization' by association of ideas with 'concert'. But the expression has acquired a fresh topicality in the current terminology of the Community where it has become a household word for the new procedures and for the complex style of the specific processes of policy-making of the Council of Ministers. Of late the Commission has taken a more critical view of the politics of concertation as practised by the Council of Ministers, and has recalled that they should be seen as a vehicle towards further integration, i.e. towards further transfers of power of decision-making, and of implementation to the institutions of the Community.

recognize explicitly the need for a preliminary involvement of all the groups and layers of a community in the discussion of policy, since their consent and co-operation is required for its implementation. But in the case of concertation it is assumed that those who take part in the making of a decision are more closely involved and committed than they are in the formal processes of consultation. In this latter case the authorities reserve the right to choose whom they want to consult, and to accept or reject their advice; while the consulted are free to follow or to desist from a particular opinion. But when the authorities practise concertation they endeavour to take direct account of the opinions of interest groups and to incorporate them and reconcile them all, in the formulation of the final policy. And the participants too are more involved in an activity in which the collaboration of all concerned is a *sine qua non* condition of the reaching of a decision. Indeed if the metaphor could be stretched further, and almost to a pun, the concertation or orchestration should include all those who are *instrumental* in the execution of a work.

THE MULTIDIMENSIONAL INTEGRATION

Mr Lawson MP (Motherwell, Lab.), said sovereignty in the sense that Parliament understood the term was already disappearing. There were sections of society with such power that they could and might render government by consent impossible. . . . These problems existed in Europe and members of the EEC would have to solve them together because they required the same kind of answers. *The Times*, 29 November 1973.

Thus at two levels, the national and the international, the discussion tried to follow the possible processes of disintegration and the possible processes of integration – and how they condition each other. While not proclaiming that the end of the nation state was inevitable, it did also recognize that the nation states themselves could prolong their 'politics' by other means but this time (unlike in Clausewitz's dictum) not by war but by peaceful integration. Of the three concepts, sovereignty, interdependence, and integration, which are bound to coexist for a long time in the contemporary political world, integration has a more global connotation. Indeed even from a semantic point of view it is rewarding to find that integration applies both to national politics, in the form of the socio-political integration required by the functioning of the modern societies, and to international politics, in the form of the supranational solution to the problems which beset the single nation states, and to the conflicts of interests which continue to oppose each one of them to the others. It is this double dialectic of integration which makes it more comprehensive. And, in general, it is more dynamic because it describes two processes linked together in a constant evolution towards greater coherence. By contrast, interdependence, which implies the balance of acquired positions, both at the national and the international level, has a more static connotation.

The discussion amounted, in general, to a mapping out of the sphere, or orbit, of real policy-making in Western Europe between its present national and supranational domains. In this respect Luxemburgensis's theory that the reduction of power of decision at the level of national sovereignty has not produced *ipso facto* an equal, or even proportionate, increase of power of decision at the supranational level is perhaps one of the most telling conclusions. The fact that the transfer of power from the allegedly declining to the allegedly emerging institutions has not been sufficiently institutionalized, is in great part responsible for the present vacuum of political power in Western Europe. This was confirmed, soon after the end of our discussion by the political problems in which Western Europe was involved during and in the light of the Middle East crisis of the autumn of 1973.

An indication of how widely realized it is that the policy-making processes of Western Europe ought to be extricated from the national-supranational no man's land can be found in the recent proposal to hold 'Summit' meetings more frequently and regularly, i.e. 'concertations' between the heads of states and/or prime ministers of the nine countries. This should be welcome: any endeavour to 'concert' with a European purpose by European policy-makers is welcome. But even if the governments of Western Europe, increasingly aware of the irreversibility of the logic of integration, were to propose integrative European solutions, the solutions run the risk of remaining inoperative. They would become operative only if they were taken and indeed prepared by 'concertation' with the European society, that is with a European public opinion thinking in European terms, through the European parliament, and with the European corporate forces (or what is called in Communitarian parlance the 'social partners') thinking in European terms through their European representations. It is this multidimensional concertation which the European Community must achieve if it is to survive. There are endless reasons, mostly belonging to the order of geo-politics or of the international economy, why European integration may not be carried to a successful end. But if there is one single major reason why European integration might falter, of the EEC's own doing, it will be its failure to communicate directly with European society.

As an individual contributor to the discussion, I have no doubt that if this kind of multidimensional integration, the only real form of integration open to modern societies, were to be brought about, it would have a positive effect on the international order. Such a European union would transform Western Europe into an internally stable and externally independent region of the world. This, in turn, would attenuate the present image of a world run by two super-powers with contrasting ideologies, and lend more credibility to the image of a world open to a plurality of influences. Finally a European union might provide a new inspiration, drawn from its coherent model of integration, to a world which is exposed to the uncertainties of the dialogue of the super-powers.

But of course, most of the contributors have expressed their own views on this general subject and may or may not agree with those put forward in these introductory notes, which must be read in this general context, and which in any case should not be separated from Karl Deutsch's concluding remarks and the rationale of integration which they outline.

Max Beloff

The Political Crisis of the European Nation-State

THE CRISIS OF THE EUROPEAN NATION-STATE IS OBVIOUSLY A
subjective notion. Objectively it would mean a complete breakdown
in the capacity of the state to provide the minimum assurances for
individual and collective endeavour and a situation in which the
choice was between total anarchy and external intervention. Such
situations have been known in some states outside Europe; it was at
the origin of the Congo crisis of 1960–61. No Western European
state has been in this situation since the re-establishment of self-
government in West Germany. Even when there has been a challenge
to a regime verging on the revolutionary as in France in 1958, the
only question was what alternative force of order would emerge to
enable the life of the French state to continue.

What we mean is something more gradual as well as more subjective. We mean a situation in which the politically conscious
elements in the community, or a large part of them, cease to believe
that the state can provide the means for meeting their legitimate
expectations and transfer their hopes and ultimately, their allegiance
to some broader unit. It is the situation that confronted the city-
states and principalities of Italy in the time of Macchiavelli. The phenomenon of a change of scale in the pattern of political organization
is indeed a recurring theme of political history, and has usually been
the product of technological change, particularly in weapons of war.

The crisis in attitude thus reflects the material world but may also
distort it. It could be that the material conditions for the nation-
state exist in Europe but that people no longer believe they do, and
therefore fail to make the best use of existing institutions, or it could
be that they are slow to appreciate the extent of change in the world
and cling to existing forms after they have ceased to function

properly. In studying the postulated crisis both aspects of the matter require attention.

The argument does not apply with equal force to all parts of the activities of the modern state. Inability to provide for military defence without entering into a system of permanent alliances with a consequent derogation from full independence in the field of foreign policy would seem to be the most obvious beginning for tendencies of this kind to develop. The industrial field would seem to be the next candidate if it is felt that the internal market of a given country together with the country's participation in international trade cannot for various reasons of scale provide the standard of living or rate of economic growth that the population feels entitled to demand of its rulers.

Since the modern state is typically interventionist in economic matters, the economy of such states will continue to be the subject of various forms of planning and control, but these functions will be exercised by authorities other than that of the nation-state. Since the economy cannot easily be divided sectorally, the authorities that control any important part of its functioning will be driven to demand control over the remainder. Of this the history of the classic federations gives ample proof. It was on the basis of the indivisibility of economic responsibilities and the primacy of these in deciding upon the real location of political sovereignty that the founders of the European Economic Community relied for the success of their enterprise.

Social policy may in part have to be integrated because of considerations arising from economic policy – avoiding distortions in competition – but will in part tend to remain for rather longer the province of the nation-state. The same is likely to be true of the nation's basic cultural institutions including the educational system, since apart from anything else, the national language is likely to be one of the key elements in the educational process.

Environmental policy, which is a relatively new concept, may be an early candidate for escaping from the control of the nation-state since the economic cost of conservation measures may demand international action if economic distortion is to be avoided. On the other hand much of private and family law may not be felt as appropriate for transfer, and the main elements of the criminal law and the general responsibility for maintaining public order and the basic substratum of an ordered society are not likely to become matters felt to be appropriate for action at any but the national level.

The history of Europe since the war would seem to suggest a highly abstract and simplified perspective of this kind as one way of marshalling events. But of course not all European states have felt the crisis to be one to the same degree; some give the appearance of having hardly felt it at all. It is also the case that contrary to the expectations of the makers of the European Community, the development has not been all one way. Some states seem to have passed through crises of confidence in which they appeared ready to surrender important elements in their hitherto sovereign powers but have then recovered and re-stated their creed of national self-sufficiency in new and seemingly acceptable terms. To some extent this is a function of size, but not in any exclusive fashion; there are both large and small states that have asserted the viability of their own national institutions and others of both kinds which have shown, or show, increasing doubts about it. Nor can a distinction in attitudes easily be drawn between countries which have some all-round economic capacity and others which are highly specialized and depend upon the international market.

Indeed the question is rather to account for the divergences in objective attitude between countries which appear to confront very similar objective situations. All European countries have had to make terms with two elements in the new situation: the overwhelming military and productive capacities of the two super-powers, and the arrival of industries whose scale of operations cannot be confined within the bounds of a national market. The main reasons for the difference in their responses can be found in the variety of their historical experiences, in particular during the second world war and the immediately subsequent period.

The European states could in this respect be divided into three main groups. There were those countries that found themselves in the area dominated by Soviet power and obliged to accept Soviet prescriptions for their internal and external behaviour. There were those who found themselves heavily dependent on American aid for their own recovery from the economic consequences of the war and upon American protection against Soviet aspirations to extend the area of Soviet domination. Finally there were the neutrals. But the neutral group must be subdivided in turn. Two of its members, Sweden and Switzerland, had such well-established polities that the whole notion of crisis seems totally inappropriate where they are concerned. Spain on the other hand had a regime that seemed so precariously rooted and so largely dependent for survival on popular reaction against the excesses of the Civil War that the word crisis seems perfectly in order; on the other hand, Spain's identification with the defeated powers and their ideologies made her an unsuitable candidate for incorporation into any wider grouping. She thus perhaps provides an example of the nation-state *malgré lui*.

The threefold classification does not eliminate certain obvious difficulties. It does not take into account the distinction just referred to between victors and vanquished, which might be presumed to have some importance in respect of people's confidence in their governments. It does not take into account the division between the two German states which has led to the creation of two nation-states experiencing the 'crisis' in two quite different ways but possibly destined to come together again, and whose attitudes towards the 'crisis' must in any event have been affected by this possibility. It does not allow for a state like Yugoslavia which has effectively asserted its national independence by resisting incorporation into the Soviet system, but which is also subject to internal pressures arising from its own multi-national composition. In some parts of Europe the nation-state is clearly the norm and it is a question of transcending it through integration into a larger unit; elsewhere the nation-state itself may not be fully developed, and we may get fission before we get fusion.

Perhaps the most important distinction that is lost is that between those nation-states that have also recently been the metropolitan territories of former imperial systems or of imperial systems in process of liquidation, and the rest. It is important to remember that a European nation-state limited in its ambitions, and even authority, to European lands alone has been exceptional in modern history, apart from countries in East-Central and South-East Europe with little or no access to maritime opportunities. Some European countries – Sweden and Denmark – had long abandoned imperial pretensions of their own; but on the eve of the second world war, Britain, France, Holland, Belgium, Italy, Portugal and even Spain, still possessed extra-European territories. And in nearly all such cases these possessions were of great importance for understanding the economic structures of the countries concerned, as well as their social structures and national outlooks. Even in the case of Germany, whose short-lived colonial empire had come to an end in 1919, the return of these colonies was among the political objectives of her government during most of the inter-war period; and Germany's claims to be an imperial power did form part of the national and nationalist creed.

The loss of imperial positions and the differing reactions to this fact in the several countries are essential to an understanding of the 'crisis' of the nation-state. One method of transcending its limitations was removed from the realm of possibility. And this made them more open to suggestions looking towards integration with their neighbours. The possibility of exercising individually an important measure of control over world commerce and world economic development disappeared. Other outlets had to be sought for their goods, their capital, and their managerial, administrative and political skills.

The energies engendered within European countries that could find no adequate expression on the domestic scene and that had hence provided the motive force behind imperial expansion had not been eliminated by the reduction in the scale of the nation's own sphere of operations. The integrationist movement could thus find human material ready to hand.

The retreat from empire was not of course a process standing on its own apart from the rise of the super-powers; it was indeed part and parcel of the same shift in the world balance. The Soviet Union contributed both by direct assistance and by example to the development of the indigenous forces of anti-colonialism at the same time as it consolidated its own non-European empire and established a new informal empire in Eastern Europe. The United States also threw its weight against the re-establishment of imperial rule in areas over-run by the Japanese and did much to encourage the withdrawal of the European powers from other areas in which they had previously exercised formal sovereignty or informal control. Sometimes by accident and sometimes by design the United States has itself replaced, at any rate for a time, the imperial powers to whose departure from the scene it contributed so much.

The influence of the super-powers is thus a manifold one. Neither the Soviet Union nor the United States suffers from the 'crisis' in the life of the nation-state; both remain in practice and in theory committed to a largely self-sustaining role. The Soviet Union imposes real derogations of sovereignty upon the countries that it dominates, but respects their sovereignty in formal terms and is committed to a belief in the general validity of the concept. The countries in the Soviet bloc make efforts to restrict the real encroachments upon their independence of action, particularly in the economic field, but proclaim a doctrine which suggests that they should subordinate their individual interests to wider tasks. The role of the nation and the nation-state is worked out in Eastern Europe largely in terms of the impact of Soviet power.

The United States is no less determined to maintain its own sovereignty, but while the Soviet Union has been wary of combinations among its neighbours, the United States has exercised its influence in favour of the integration of Western Europe and the supersession in that area of the historic nation-state. This pressure has both assisted and hindered the realization of the 'European' idea. The countries of Western Europe for their part define their own position in respect of nationhood largely in terms of their feeling towards the United States, which at once protects them militarily and assists them economically but threatens to overwhelm them culturally.

Were it not for this fundamental ambivalence in their attitude to the United States and particularly to the expressions of its economic strength – notably the so-called multinational companies – the problem might have been a simpler one. Because of the dependence of Western Europe upon the Americans for purposes of defence and because of the penetration of their economies by American interests it is by no means clear that the crisis of the nation-state in Europe can be solved by a transfer of powers to institutions limited to Europe. On the other hand, integration on an 'Atlantic' basis cannot seriously be contemplated while the United States itself is under no such internal pressure to abandon its sovereignty.

It is also not clear to what extent the new European structure can generalize and remove from direct national participation the relationship of its member countries with the former colonial world. Can the frustrated paternalism that finds its expression in aid programmes be torn out of its national context and made effective through European institutions? Or is it more likely that the survival of particular links between ex-colonial powers and their former possessions will help to keep alive a sense of national differences of interest and outlook and thus perpetuate the ideology of the nation-state.

Historical parallels, while they illuminate some of the problems under discussion, do not much help in their solution. Where political units have proved too small in the past the upshot has been the forcible imposition of new structures; the nation-states of today are as often as not the outcome of Bismarckian 'blood and iron', not of the voluntary transcendence of divisions through consent. Even the Swiss cantons do not provide unequivocal evidence in the opposite direction. Nor, on the other hand, do we know what the increased speed and density of communications may do towards assisting in solving through international action what would otherwise need to be done through supra-national authority. The logic of the integrationists – through economics to politics – is plausible enough but it has yet to be demonstrated. One may be writing off the nation-state all too soon.

Léon Dion

Anti-Politics and Marginals

AMONG ACADEMICS, ESPECIALLY IN AMERICA, A PSEUDO-THEORY OF stable democracies has recently been developed and there is keen competition to invent indices which grade countries according to a scale which runs from the highest possible degree of stability to the greatest instability.[1] And yet our stable democracies are only a hundred to a hundred and fifty years old – a mere moment in the long history of mankind.

The title-deeds upon which the claims to greatness of contemporary liberal democracies are based are many and genuine; they are advanced industrial economies, which promise, if mankind so desires, opportunities for productivity which will give a completely new meaning to the ideas of 'scarcity', of the distribution of economic wealth and services and to the idea of work itself; allegiance to lofty, humanist values founded on the affirmation of the primacy of the individual as a citizen; pride of place given to individual rights as contrasted with the corporatist rights of *anciens régimes*, which oppressed the individual and paralysed social and economic growth; toleration of non-conformist ideas and movements; flexibility in dealing with conflicts between individuals and groups. These characteristics of the regimes of liberal democracies and other similar regimes amount to the affirmation of the freedom of individuals and of associations, often embodied in laws or in charters of the rights of man and of the citizen; to the recognition of pluralistic values and of the plurality of social groups, the right to political opposition, pro-

---

[1] The United States generally heads the list, although in a study based on the 'index of democratic performance' the United States came only sixteenth, Great Britain being first, followed by France which is usually thought to be an unstable democracy. See: Deane E. Neubauer, 'Some Conditions of Democracy', *The American Political Review*, Vol. 16, No. 4, 1967, pp. 1002–9.

vided that it is loyal, that is, that it respects the liberal creed and expresses itself through appropriate channels.

During the 1950s, the polyarchic formula, which took for granted the unconditional adherence of individuals and groups to majority rule insofar as it assumed that there was no permanent majority or minority on any particular question, seemed to be about to take root in a great many liberal democracies. Vast changes took place at all levels of society, but the liberal democracies seemed to be able to absorb the shock of these changes to their structures and outlook. So great was this enthusiasm and fervour that some people began to proclaim 'the end of ideologies'. In domestic politics, at least, conflicts between individuals and groups seemed to have died down to such an extent that it seemed quite natural to believe that the great liberal dream of universal harmony was about to come true. Today we know how artificial were the economic prosperity and social peace of those years and how unfitted was the machinery of the welfare state to carry out in time the readjustments which changed circumstances and aspirations required. All these high hopes, in fact, vanished as if by magic from one day to the next and nothing has been able to stem the rise in radical contestation within the liberal democracies during the last six or seven years. Appearing first in the United States, the most 'advanced' country in the world, revolt spread like wild-fire in Japan, France, Britain, Italy and affected nearly all social groups, although it was strongest among the youth and some categories of underprivileged in the cities and outlying provinces. Our proud democracies had considered themselves above such ills, which were the lot of South American and Afro-Asian countries only. They believed that only the residue of former ills, which time would heal, survived within them: ills such as electoral abstentionism or the obduracy with which some social categories refused to profit from the opportunities offered to them to better themselves.

How can we account for this change of attitude which took place in such a short time? Interpretations abound: sociologists, anthropologists, psychologists, and political scientists have all put forward learned suggestions, which are all valid up to a point. But too often there is a tendency to pass over in silence the first explanation which springs to mind, which is that the performance of our societies during the last six or seven years has been far from brilliant and even, in some fundamental respects, has declined. In spite of vast opportunities which should have ensured the constant growth of the rhythm of economic expansion, technology has ceased to renew itself and the lack of innovation has been only too obvious. The most advanced societies flounder in the vicious circles, which they cannot break, of galloping inflation and high unemployment. The inequalities between continents, peoples, even between social classes and regions in the same society continually increase, instead of disappearing. It is not, however, economic and social inequality in itself but the feeling that those in power are not doing enough to remedy it, or even that they are powerless to do so, in spite of their good intentions, which is becoming increasingly hard for a growing number of individuals and groups to bear. It is the existing cogs and systems which are most sharply criticized. The archaic character of the political apparat is resented and the weakness of most of the secondary social institutions, especially the political parties and interest groups is deplored.

This is not the place to put the political parties, national assemblies, bureaucracies, judicial institutions and police forces, and governments on trial once again. In those aspects which deal most closely with the smooth running of modern society, I have shown how inadequate, not to say inept, they are.[2] The machine is unable to respond to the demands made upon it – demands which are more and more discordant and pressing, nor can it cope with problems which daily become more complex and more numerous. There is a chronic risk that it will choke and overheat or, to use Michel Crozier's expression, become blocked.[3]

Leaving aside the cogs and the systems, the plane of values is often turned into a battleground. Contrary to what is often stated, this is less an attempt to recreate values than a reproach levelled against the men and the systems in power for their failure to act according to the values in which they claim to believe (liberty, equality, human dignity, etc.) or again, for their inability to redefine and adjust these values to the demands of the present. We are faced with a mounting tide of disillusionment. Thus I have written elsewhere:[4]

[2] See on this subject my explanation in *Société et politique: la vie des groupes*. Volume 1: *Fondements de la société libérale*; Volume 2; *Dynamique de la société libérale*, Presses de l'Université Laval, 1971, 1972 and, with particular reference to Quebec, *La prochaine révolution*, Editions Leméac, Montreal, 1973.

[3] Note, however, that contrary to Michel Crozier who says that French society is blocked, I merely say of liberal democracies that if things go on as they are, they will become blocked. Between these two ways of looking at the question, there is more than a mere nuance; there is the indication of a different approach to the analysis of societies.

[4] *Société et politique: la vie des groupes*, Volume 2, *Dynamique de la société libérale*, *op. cit.*, pp. 469–70.

What is called in question today is not some dysfunctionings in the social and political systems which, when all is said and done, are easily remedied. The crisis extends to the legitimacy of the organizations and leaders; to the integration of its members in the political system; to the involvement of its members in the life of the organizations, to the rules and processes which decide how goods and services are to be shared between individuals and collectivities. In short, it questions the essential purposes of men and of society. The challenge is at the very level of the values, of their nature, of their institutionalization and of their interiorization. What contestation expresses, often brutally and clumsily, is the anguish of men and collectivities faced with a world which has become unfamiliar and frightening. It expresses also a longing for liberation, for purification and for creativity: it is, in short, the longing for a new humanism. The hippy, the drug-addict, the teenage drop-out, the adult who throws up a successful career are all symptoms of a world which is losing its soul. The revolt in the American universities against behaviourism and quantitative methods, and the recent popularity, especially among students, of religious courses, allied with great interest in ancient and exotic religions, the practice of the harshest asceticism and mystical experiments of every kind among circles which are officially said to be dissolute, and, on the other hand, the sudden and apparently irreversible rise of reactionary and repressive impulses among those who only yesterday were the main upholders of liberal values are all too clear signs of the depth of the crisis and the fatal outcome which threatens.

Two thousand five hundred years of apparently thoughtful application of the human mind to the task of making societies more governable – to take only western civilization – has not succeeded in banishing the temptation to refuse to serve from assailing individuals and collectivities. Dormant for long periods, the spirit of rebellion at other times awakes, often for obscure reasons, and sometimes it has only been appeased after great social upheavals. It seems that our own age is marked out for rebellion.

The symptoms of this diagnosis are many and irrefutable. Thus, if one observes the functioning of the mechanism of social and political interaction (the political parties, the interest groups, the communications media and the consultative councils), it is clear that they have not succeeded in channelling towards the political system many of the more pressing demands made by individuals and

collectivities. They either turn a deaf ear to them or fail to direct them
into political channels. Understandably enough, these demands are
largely concerned with values and ideologies, since the machinery
for interaction has become such a poor ideological vessel, but they
also concern many other aspects of economic and social life.

This has two consequences. Firstly, strong social aspirations or
pressing social problems find no outlet in political terms, so that
political life is sadly impoverished and there is widespread social
stagnation. This is a common situation, which has often been clinic-
ally examined. And, secondly, many collective aspirations and social
problems, in order to find political expression, look for and find
channels outside the machinery of institutional interaction. This is
why the liberal democracies have come to differ very little from this
point of view from dictatorial regimes, such as the Paraguayan, for
instance, where, because of the non-acceptance of political forms of
opposition, an institution like the Catholic Church plays the role of a
para-party or perhaps even better, of a quasi-pressure group for the
mass of the people who are oppressed and deprived of institutional
means of political expression.

This is why, even in liberal democracies in which the right to
dissent is recognized and in which there exists machinery to channel
opposition movements into the political system, as well as the possibility, provided some not very restrictive rules are observed, of setting up new opposition groups if the need thereof is felt, new parallel
socio-political networks or cogs are established which are used by
greater or lesser numbers of people: citizens' committees, community
organizations, political clubs, common fronts, 'operations' of every
kind, some of which assume permanent structures, as, for example,
the *'Operations-dignité'* in Quebec, etc. Either these networks or cogs
are willing, sooner or later, to act within the existing system and thus
to perform a work of salvage so that they are sooner or later
recognized by political agencies as mechanisms for institutional interaction, or they can refuse to work within the existing political system
and so become marginal or even subversive. These differentiations in
the orientation of compensatory machinery in relation to the existing
political system are very important. To understand them and to
appreciate their whole political import, it is essential not to confine
the analysis within the existing political system but to conduct it
along the lines of the political system of reference which can be, de-
pending on the individuals or collectivities concerned, either the
existing system or a different system.

Any research into these multiple and various parallel cogs must first deal with the elementary, but essential, problem of classification. This is why I have distinguished between organic collectivities, which are officially recognized by the existing political system and non-organic collectivities, which operate without official recognition, that is, which can be ignored or even banned by the political authorities. Furthermore, within each of these types, the collectivities divide according to their degree of acceptance or rejection, conditional or unconditional, of the existing system.[5] These conditions can be reproduced as follows:

Degree of institutionalization of collectivities

Legal status	Position in relation to the existing political system	
	Conditional	Unconditional
Organic		
Non-organic		

Moreover, the methods used by the groups can be either integrative, that is to say recognized and accepted by the existing political system, or they may be divisive, and thus considered as reprehensible, or even subversive, by the system. If one places integration and divisiveness along a continuum, one can classify the means of action as follows: the fulfilling of public roles; the active support of political agents, as for example, taking part in consultative councils; agreeing to negotiate peacefully with political agents over differences; simple lobbying, fall on the side of integration, and the resort to ordinary manifestations (petitions, marches, etc.), intimidation, obstruction, terrorism, revolt, and revolution, fall on the side of divisiveness.[6]

One must distinguish between the character – organic or non-organic – of a collectivity and the means of action – integrative or divisive – it employs, since the former stresses the ends pursued, while the second falls back on the methods or resources employed. Thus a non-organic movement can pursue ends which are entirely acceptable to the system, while at the same time it is condemned by

---

[5] On this point, see: Léon Dion and Micheline de Sève, *Cultures politiques au Québec, Document de travail théorique,* 1972 (mimeographed).

[6] See: *Société et politique: la vie des groupes,* Vol. 2, *op. cit.,* p. 252.

the system because of the destructive means of action it employs; nevertheless, it must be remembered that some movements, which pursue ends which are completely admissible according to contemporary humanist standards, may justifiably turn to divisive action, if the political system remains obdurately deaf to their appeals.

In order to illustrate how collectivities which do not have an outlet can be led to become, or to remain, non-organic (conditionally or unconditionally) and to turn to divisive means of action, I have chosen Canada, which has the reputation of being a very liberal country and so, presumably, very tolerant of opposition movements. From among many possible instances, I have chosen to comment very briefly on the *Front de libération du Québec*, the committees for political action, the '*Opérations-dignité*' of Bas-du-Fleuve and Gaspésie, the unrest aroused by the adoption of a draft bill on the promotion of the French language in Quebec (Bill 63) and, more generally, the behaviour of the Canadian political system when faced with the claims to autonomy of Quebec during the last ten years.

The *Front de libération du Québec* (FLQ) is a terrorist movement born at the very beginning of the upsurge of the separatist movement in Quebec at the beginning of the last decade. Having made itself known by means of *graffiti* and threats addressed to politicians and industrialists, the movement then claimed the responsibility for several bomb attacks. In June 1963, a bomb exploded at dawn in a letter-box in the centre of Montreal. One man was killed and another was crippled for life in trying to defuse another bomb, which had been placed in a second letter-box, not far from the first. In October 1970, the FLQ achieved world wide fame by kidnapping and holding for weeks on end the British diplomat, James Cross, and by kidnapping and murdering the Quebec Minister, Pierre Laporte. Its aim is the destruction of the Canadian political system and of capitalism. It desires a sovereign and socialist Quebec state. Convinced that it will be impossible to attain these ends by the methods and means of action recognized by the present liberal democratic system (parties and elections, parliamentary opposition, resort to the usual pressure techniques, majority rule), it has turned to every conceivable kind of violence. The FLQ is thus an unconditional non-organic movement which systematically uses extremely divisive methods.

The *Comités d'action politique* (CAP), which exist primarily in the metropolitan area of Montreal, stem from the citizens' committees which have proliferated in Quebec since 1964. Extending to the whole of political life the concerns of the latter, which concentrated on particular questions (housing, medical services, etc.), the CAP in Montreal, after the National Confederation of Trade Unions (CSN) had opened a 'second front' in 1968 (*front politique*), regrouped themselves into a semi-federation called the *Front d'action politique* (FRAP) and carried the struggle into the city by challenging the mayor, M. Drapeau and his civic 'party' in the 1970 elections. Associated in the public mind with the FLQ which at the time was kidnapping Cross and assassinating Laporte, and disposing anyhow of very limited resources, compared with the organization of Mayor Drapeau, the FRAP was humiliatingly defeated in the elections, and faced with all kinds of difficulties and internal dissension, it faded away into embryonic existence. By contrast, the CAP, especially in Saint-Jacques and Maisonneuve continue to expand, but after the crushing defeat of 1970 may have been driven to become increasingly revolutionary. It can therefore be said that the FRAP was conditionally organic and used integrative methods. In effect, though it advocated a radical change in the municipal government of Montreal, it nevertheless accepted the rules of the electoral game by putting up candidates for vacant places on the municipal council. The CAP, on the other hand, no longer believe that it is possible for them to win by observing the rules of the game of the existing municipal system and, professing faith in Marxism, they remain unconditional and non-organic. But, in spite of their scepticism about integrative methods, they confine themselves to encouraging the class struggle, while persistently refusing to turn to superior divisive methods (such as sabotage and terrorism). This is what distinguishes them from the FLQ.

The case of the '*Operations-dignité*', to which should be added that of the cardboard industry of Cabano, since both involve the same region (the Bas-Saint-Laurent and the Gaspésie), and the same people (priests, notables, deputies, fishermen, farmers and woodcutters) and both are concerned with socio-economic developments, although differing greatly from the first two examples, is similarly instructive. Here one finds a regrouping of men whom the delays and ineffectiveness of official, political and administrative procedures had rendered so impatient that they decided to take matters into their own hands, with the help of councillors whom they themselves had elected. The requisite funds came from the respective governments, but they are administered by a private non-profit-making organization, the Forestry Research Foundation of Laval University. It was with this Foundation and not with the appropriate governmental bodies that those responsible for the '*Operations-dignité*' signed the protocol of agreement. Until now, their methods have been integrative (lobbying, petitions, marches, and the usual demonstrations) but if pressed too hard they could easily adopt more divisive procedures (as they did in Cabano). The '*Operations-dignité*' represent a type of conditional non-organic organization, which could easily change into an unconditional organic movement. On the surface all is quiet. But let us not be deceived. The conditions prefiguring the possibility of an easy and swift passage to the unconditional non-organic movement are well and truly present. One isolated incident could spark off the use of extreme divisive methods, for the degree of frustration and discontent among the people has already reached a high potential of violence. But for this to happen there would have to be a change in the present leadership.

In the autumn of 1969, the Quebec government, then led by Jean-Jacques Bertrand, head of the *Union Nationale*, tabled a bill (63) 'to foster the use of the French language in Quebec',[7] which immediately provoked a very powerful wave of opposition among the students, professors and intellectuals generally, who thought that the bill was a step towards the assimilation of French to English rather than a measure to protect the French language. In spite of many noisy demonstrations and numerous articles and reports in the press and on radio and television, almost the whole National Assembly, the members of the liberal opposition as well as the governmental party, refused to heed the protests. They denounced them as the work of 'leftists', 'revolutionaries', and 'dreamers'. Only four or five deputies from both parties, making up what was called at the time the 'circumstantial opposition', opposed the bill outright and echoed the dramatic arguments which took place outside the precincts of the National Assembly. But the echo was too faint and could not realize the hopes of the oppositionists. It was then that the oppositional forces began openly to proclaim and to write that, in the circumstances, 'real' political legitimacy was to be found in the streets and not in parliament, and that the deputies were traitors to their mandate which bound them to protect the national heritage and therefore, although they had been elected democratically, they did not 'represent' the will of the 'real' people. The bill was finally passed by an overwhelming majority of both parties, after a month of

[7] A similar bill had been tabled, the previous autumn, but it had to be withdrawn, after a wave of protests during the debates of the parliamentary commission set up to discuss the project, and also among the general public.

debate and substantial amendments, proposed by the leader of the liberal opposition, Jean Lesage, but it is still the object of bitter hostility among intellectuals and, more recently, the trade unions. It is very probable that the liberal government of Robert Bourassa, after the Report of the Commission of Inquiry on the promotion of the French language published at the beginning of 1973, will withdraw or radically modify this law before launching into new elections. It is difficult to classify this oppositional movement to a proposed law. But if, for example, one compares it to another bill, which was equally hotly debated (Bill 60), which proposed to set up a Ministry of Education and a Higher Council of Education (June 1963–March 1964), a debate in which all the protagonists were officially recognized and which was channelled and to some extent conducted by the Prime Minister, Jean Lesage,[8] one can see great differences. While the opposition aroused by Bill 60 was unconditionally organic and many of the suggestions put forward by individuals and associations during the debate were incorporated in the final text of the law, the opposition engendered by Bill 63 was nonorganic, at least insofar as neither the government nor the deputies were willing to recognize it or to treat with it and insofar as the demonstrators who had regrouped themselves into the *Front du Québec français* began to question the legitimacy of the deputies seated in the National Assembly. One may consider this movement as having been by force of circumstances (that is by the will of the government and deputies) non-organic, but in such a way as to have been certainly conditional.

When, towards 1960, the first great demonstrations of a new wave of separatism appeared in Quebec, especially with the Marcel Chaput affair, the governments of Canada and of Quebec decided to adopt a permissive attitude and left the movement to develop along its own lines. Very few liberal countries, in similar circumstances, would have adopted the same attitude. Now after more than ten years have gone by, it is clear that this same attitude, though it has not prevented the rise of terrorist organizations, has certainly prevented them from winning over the support of large sections of the population. But it has not been able to stem the rise of the separatist current, which after many divagations, has finally been transformed into a respectable and powerful political party, the *Parti Québécois*. In the provincial elections of April 1970 it won 24 per cent of the popular

[8] On this question, see my book: *Le bill 60 et la société québécoise*, HMH, Montreal, 1967.

vote although it succeeded in winning only four departments out of 108. The *Parti Québécois* now hopes to increase still further its share of the popular vote in the next elections and, with the help of a more advantageous electoral map, to win them. It is a perfect example of a conditional organic movement, using integrative means of action.

A host of other examples illustrating this argument can be drawn from the Canadian experience, each of them showing the inability of the Canadian and Quebec governments to acknowledge certain categories of demands put forward by individuals and groups, to articulate them and to translate them into appropriate actions and decisions.

At first sight, the Canadian government might seem to have behaved admirably towards the separatist movement in Quebec. Indeed, by allowing the movement to spread freely and even by giving it official recognition, the government has proved that it adheres firmly to liberal values, without any of the shabby restrictions and dodges with which so many other governments can be reproached. But should the Weimar Republic be congratulated for having handed itself over lock, stock, and barrel to the National Socialists? And what conclusion should be drawn from the fact that the efforts made since 1963 to combat the separatist threat have dealt only with the secondary aspects of the problem and have failed to deal with essentials? In the short run, Canada, of all the western democracies, is the most immediately threatened by internal upheaval. And, above all, what can one say of the refusal of the federal authorities to grant Quebec its right to political self-determination, a right representing for the people of Quebec the guarantee which they demand in growing numbers, above all since the federal government reintroduced emergency measures and since the military 'occupation' of October 1970.

In the case of the draft bill 63, the Quebec government quite simply refused to initiate the dialogue so ardently desired by a considerable part of the population for whom the linguistic question is of the utmost importance, both in itself and for the collectivity, and who considered themselves competent enough to have their opinion taken into account. The short-sighted electoral aims, the proven dependence on powerful private interests, and the cowardice in relation to the English-speaking people of the Quebec government and parliament quite unnecessarily caused the students, teachers, and intellectuals to withdraw, often for good, the confidence they had hitherto had in the political system.

Though it finds expression in different ideologies and methods, the message of '*Operations-dignité*', the CAP, and the FLQ is fundamentally the same: it concerns individual and collective equality, social justice, respect for the individual and the quest for greater autonomy. These are admirable objectives which the political authorities admire and themselves claim to pursue. The Manifesto of October 1970 of the FLQ, which was read over the television in most dramatic circumstances,[9] made a profound impression precisely because it stressed the injustices which the weak and helpless have to face daily in their work, their environment and their general way of life. The message of the twenty priests of Bas-du Fleuve and Gaspésie, which was published a few weeks later, but which had been written much earlier, took up the same theme again in more restrained terms. Even the letter of the Assembly of Bishops of Quebec, addressed to the newspapers at the height of the events of October, contained the same theme of 'peace with justice'.

It is understandable enough that the government should repress the violent actions of the *Front de libération du Québec*, that it should be chary of the CAP which are Marxist and are fighting for the destruction of the capitalist social and economic system, and that it should be circumspect with regard to '*Operations-dignité*' which, in their pursuit of a social rationality, often lose sight of economic rationality. What one is at a loss to understand and would very much like to, is the inability of politicians, despite their evident good will, to formulate and to put into effect courageous national and social policies which, by going to the roots of the evil, would eradicate the conditions which feed discontent among the underprivileged in the towns and the populations of the outlying regions.

These illustrations have been drawn from Canada, but they could just as well have been drawn from other countries and they show clearly how and to what extent the 'marginals', owing to deficiencies in the political system, are led to take the path of 'anti-politics'. Yet it must not be thought that governments are powerless and fated to do nothing when faced with these dissident tendencies,

---

[9] One of the conditions demanded by the kidnappers of James Cross was that before he was released, the Manifesto should be read over Radio Canada. This was the only condition which the Canadian government, for clear 'humanitarian' reasons, accepted. In June of the same year the *Front de libération de Québec* had sent the text of a similar communication to the radio and television stations, but to our knowledge, it was only printed in one newspaper, *Québec-Presse* and did not give rise to any comment.

some of which threaten the integrity of the country and attack the basis of liberal regimes. On the contrary, they have to hand vast reserves of sanctions (rewards and punishments) which they can use to win the support of individuals and collectivities, to coax and silence the recalcitrant. One does not change the political system just as one swops one's old Ford for a new car. One must also take into account the capacity of political systems to adjust to change and their ability, which is sometimes astonishing, to absorb non-organic orientations and, by legitimizing them, to prevent divisive ways and means of action from damaging the continued existence of the system.

Micheline de Sève and I wrote on this subject in an unpublished text designed to base the study of political culture on firm theoretical foundations:

Unless a political system has already suffered such assaults that one may clearly stand up to it with impunity, one can take for granted that the reasons which make individuals and collectivities conform to the will of the political forces are far more imperative than the motives which would make them disobey. Even those who unconditionally reject the political system are obliged, to some extent, to submit to the law of that system. The examination of their assessment of the political situation, of their organization for political action and of the aims of their political action will reveal to what extent the aims of the political system as well as the methods of 'persuasion' which it employs condition the forms which rejection, revolt, or apathy adopt.

Man, however, has an indestructible will (and it is one of the characteristics upon which his greatness is based), no matter how vacillating and erratic it may be, to overcome all the circumstances which seem to him to be the source of evil. If the analysis is to be valid, it is not enough to reconstitute the way in which the needs of the system condition the assessment of political purposes. The analysis must also pay as much attention to non-organic dispositions as to organic ones. But one must go further. One must include in one's field of vision the efforts made to create radical or revolutionary movements, and make an effort to evaluate their political significance. Again, one must examine the embryonic political structures created by some collectivities. To avoid the systematic illusion to which the analyst is liable (the belief that analysis can only reveal processes, actions and decisions which are impelled by the system) instead of making the actual political system the object of analysis, we should rather concentrate on the system of reference. It does not matter if it is presented in an imaginary ideal, partially actualized, borrowed, partial or complete, homogeneous or heteroclite form. In an analysis of political culture we should pay equal attention to all the assessments, no matter what their framework of systemic reference may be.[10]

In spite of the astonishing ease with which western liberal societies have managed to avoid or repel the many attacks made on them in recent times, it would be foolhardy to believe that they can continue to do so indefinitely. They are no more assured of immortality than were the societies which went before them. Only major adjustments in the functioning of the political apparatus and a radical revision of goals can conjure away the danger.[11] We should remember that it is the failure of politics which makes the bed for revolutions.

Translated from French

[10] Léon Dion and Micheline de Sève, *Les cultures politiques au Québec* (Document théorique), pp. 81–2.

[11] I have tried to point out the extent of the necessary readjustments in the conclusions to *Société et politique: la vie des groupes*, PUL, Quebec, Volume 2, pp. 457–89.

Dennis Kavanagh

Beyond Autonomy?
The Politics of Corporations

IN RECENT YEARS THERE HAS BEEN A FORMIDABLE GROWTH OF literature on the political and other implications of business corporations. Much of the writing on the corporations has been of an alarmist nature. We are usually referred to the growth of an impressive economic (and, by implication, political) power of the corporations, the lack of effective democratic control on their activities, and the consequent need to establish a more effective set of constraints. It is suggested that internally the corporations are tending to by-pass the legislatures and other representative institutions, while externally the multinationals are integrating sectors of economies across states, and employing a management which may owe primary loyalty to the corporation and not the state in which managers are based.[1] The emergence of the 'multinationals therefore not only seriously challenges many of our cherished political institutions and procedures, it also confronts our patterns of thinking about the sovereign state which have been inherited from the 16th century. In that they escape from the constraints of national boundaries and representative institutions it is alleged that the corporations are rendering obsolescent our traditional concepts of both state and sovereignty. Much of this argument is neatly encapsulated in the evocative titles of such scholarly works as *Beyond the Nation State* and *Sovereignty at Bay*.

There is now wide recognition that many advanced industrial states are undergoing a third industrial revolution or a post-industrial revolution, which is essentially international in scope and technological in basis.[2] This has indeed produced an asymmetry

---

[1] For some corporations' statements to this effect see Christopher Tugendhat, *The Multinationals*, Eyre & Spottiswoode, London, 1971, pp. 4-5.

[2] 'In the sixteenth century framework [of thinking] the international corporation is an intruder'. Hugh Stephenson, *The Coming Clash*, Weidenfeld & Nicolson, London, 1972.

between the international reach of business and the essentially national organization of governments and other groups.[3] Hence the prospects for contradictions between industrial societies and the nation states which contain them open up. It is these tensions which this paper wants to explore, particularly as they relate to the issues of autonomy, sovereignty and peace.

Are the corporations a threat to national sovereignty? If so, are they a force for supranational institutions and arrangements? Again, if this is the case, will it make the world a more peaceful place?

The view expressed here is that much of the discussion about the decline or loss of sovereignty is ill-informed and highly speculative. In its classic usage the term sovereignty clearly refers to the ultimate power to decide on political matters and to enforce decisions; it means that sovereign states, for example, are separate and supreme in deciding on constitutional issues within their territories. Whether that power is shared among different centres (as in a federation), or whether it is actually exercised, or whether the sovereign power finds itself confronted by counter-pressures and constraints are other issues. In its constitutional usage sovereignty is a distinct question from the effectiveness of government *vis-à-vis* other groups and also from the general question of the governability of a society. It is worth defending this view because discussions of such features as the interdependence of states, the growth of international actors like multinational corporations, and the crude projection of recent socio-economic trends all too easily elide into a statement of the erosion of a carelessly or ill-defined concept of sovereignty. Of course the autonomy of governments has been limited, particularly in the military and economic spheres; this feature, however, has not detracted from the supreme ultimate and legal rights which states enjoy to make their own decisions. Individual states are still the major actors in world politics and are likely to remain so in the foreseeable future. As Alan James has argued, in the course of a forceful defence of the relevance of national sovereignty, 'Interdependence has not destroyed constitutional independence. The separate sovereign state has by no means withered away.'[4]

---

[3] This is better conveyed in Aron's reference to *industrial societies*, which alerts us to both the centripetal and the centrifugal tendencies, than in Galbraith's notion of *industrial states*.

[4] Alan James, 'The Contemporary Relevance of National Sovereignty', in Michael Leifer, ed., *Constraints and Adjustments in British Foreign Policy*, London, 1972.

It goes without saying that there is no ideal-type corporation or state and that there are hardly any typical relationships between them, or between the parent and the subsidiaries in the multinational corporations.[5] The task of generalizing is made difficult because we need to distinguish among: (a) states which differ in the intactness of their sovereignties; (b) corporations which differ according to whether their shareholdings are privately-owned, state-owned, or a mixture of both; (c) multinational organizations which differ according to how international and how integrated their activities are.[6] (Management attitudes may be primarily geocentric (in which the company takes a global view of its activities), ethnocentric (in which management assumes and carries out the view of the parent body in the subsidiaries), or polycentric (in which management assumes the view of the host country wherever the enterprise is based)[7]); (d) states which differ in the extent and form of their penetration by foreign investment; (e) states which differ in their interpretations of sovereignty and finally (f) government – corporation inter-relationships which differ according to the varying social, cultural, and economic backgrounds of the states.

The relations between corporations and states raise interesting questions for conventional political science, concerning particularly its subject-matter and the boundaries within and between the disciplines. One might argue, in parentheses, that the interface of government and corporation – crossing the boundaries of politics and economics – provides a vantage-point for a genuine study of political economy.[8] Such a focus meets the contemporary demand

[5] For a sample of discussions on this point see Raymond Vernon, *Sovereignty at Bay*, Longmans, London, 1971, and the contributions to John H. Dunning, ed., *The Multinational Enterprise*, Allen & Unwin, London, 1971.

[6] For a sample of discussions on this point see Raymond Vernon, *op. cit.*, and the contributions to John H. Dunning, *op. cit.*

[7] For discussion of different management styles see the following, Michael A. Brooke and H. Lee Remmers, *The Strategy of Multinational Enterprise*, Longmans, London, 1970; Robert J. Alsegg, *Control Relationships Between American Corporations and their European Subsidiaries*, American Management Association, Inc., New York, 1971; and Howard V. Parlmutter, 'Unions and Firms as Worldwide Institutions', in Hans Gunter, *Transnational Industrial Relations*, Macmillan, London, 1972.

[8] 'The Rise of the Managed Economy Reunites Politics and Economics with a Truly Political Economy', A. Cairncross, *The Managed Economy*, Blackwell, 1970, and for an early statement, see Robert A. Dahl, 'Business and Politics: A Critical Appraisal of Political Science', in Dahl *et al.*, eds., *Social Science Research on Business: Product Potential*, Columbia University Press, New York, 1959.

for greater 'relevance' in the subject-matter of political science and the appeal that research should not be confined to the study of formal governmental or political institutions but should attend also to the public impact of overtly 'private' groups. On this criterion the corporations, 'the new Principalities' according to Dahl,[9] or 'states' according – to A. A. Berle,[10] become pre-eminent candidates for political analysis.[11] The very size and resource-base of such a company as General Motors unbalances any pluralistic polity and enables it to make many key decisions affecting its own environment. By reason of their decisions affecting investment, prices and salaries, location of plant and employment, the corporations are engaged in the authoritative allocation of values for the public.

In addition, there is the challenge to existing boundaries within political science which stems from the explosive growth of inter-relationships across state borders. Increasingly, we are aware that exogenous factors, or the international environment, affect the political dynamics within a state and that state borders are unable to insulate peoples, economies, and ideas from these influences. David Easton has provided a useful perspective with the analytic distinction he draws between the political system and its environment,[12] as has James Rosenau with his notion of 'linkage politics'[13]; these latter include those acts of transnational penetration and reaction which link the national and the international political systems.

Four features of the modern mature corporation which are relevant to this paper are: first, *its massive size*. The annual sales turnover of such corporate giants such as GM, Unilever, IBM, ITT, Standard

[9] Robert A. Dahl, *After the Revolution*, Yale University Press, New Haven, 1971.

[10] A. A. Berle, *The Three Faces of Power*, Harcourt Brace, New York, 1968.

[11] Other writers would also be happier to view the giant corporations as 'states'. For an elaborated analogy of the corporation to the state see Earl Latham, 'The Body Politik of the Corporation', in E. S. Mason, ed., *The Corporation in Modern Society*, Atheneum, Cambridge, Mass., 1959. For example, General Motors, with its 1·3 million stockholders, 800,000 employees, operating in twenty-four states, and with an annual turnover exceeding that of the GNP of most states, may more plausibly be regarded as a miniature political system than a 'mere' commercial enterprise or pressure group.

[12] Cf. David Easton, *A Systems Analysis of Political Life*, Wiley, New York, 1965, pp. 21 f.

[13] James Rosenau, *Linkage Politics*, Free Press, New York, 1969. Linkage politics is defined by Rosenau as 'any recurrent sequence of behaviour that originates in one system and is reacted to in another', *op. cit.*, p. 45.

Oil and Ford exceed the GNP's of many states. Size is important in enabling an enterprise to reap the economies of large-scale production, support high risk investment and expensive research and development (R & D), employ a large stock of skilled personnel, make long-range plans and increase bargaining and market power.[14] These 'imperatives' have encouraged a spate of mergers within and across states. Of the largest one hundred economic units in the world fifty are states and fifty are multinational enterprises and, in the United States, concentration has proceeded to the point where the 200 largest US corporations control two-thirds of US manufacturing assets.[15]

Second, *its specialization*. The above analysis applies *a fortiori*, to the technology-based industries such as computers, oil, automobiles, chemicals, steel, and aero-space. These products tend to require high R & D costs and most are homogeneous enough to be produced almost anywhere; such industries are marked by oligopoly at home, and, for the first four sectors, by the establishment of overseas subsidiaries.[16]

Third, *the symbiosis of state and industry*. Governments, like the corporations, are interested in developing a predictable and planned market, and their policies for the regulation of aggregate demand, prices and incomes, tariffs, and the role of the state as investor in and purchaser of advanced technological products (particularly in computers, aero-space and defence) are all signs of this partnership. The bulk of the scientific research performed by industrial firms in most industrial states is financed by the government. Galbraith has termed this symbiosis of state and industry 'The New Industrial State'.

Fourth, *the autonomy of technostructure or specialist staff*. According to some commentators leadership in industrial society is now found in

[14] These economies of scale do not necessarily apply to all enterprises. In less technological industries the evidence suggests that large size does not correlate with level of profits. For a review of the evidence see John Child. *The Business Enterprise in Modern Industrial Society*, Collier–Macmillan, London, 1969, pp. 95–7.

[15] For a useful summary of the trends and figures for corporate mergers and concentration in America see Richard J. Barber, *The American Corporation*, MacGibbon Kee, London, 1970, Chap. 2. More generally, and controversially, see J. K. Galbraith, *The New Industrial State*, Penguin, London, 1967.

[16] For instance some 40 per cent of the value of direct US investment in West Germany and Britain is accounted for by three multinationals, Standard Oil, General Motors and Ford. See Galbraith, *op. cit.*, Chaps. 26, 27 and Shonfield, *Modern Capitalism*, Oxford University Press, London, 1965.

the technostructure (the experts and the salaried managers).[17] This has arisen as a result of the divorce of ownership from managerial control and the need for complex long-range planning. In capitalist societies the technostructure is concerned to assert its autonomy from both public and market controls, and in communist states there is evidence that these same managers are gaining influence at the expense of party leaders and bureaucrats.[18] This development approximates to Saint-Simon's vision of a future industrial society, a society which would be international and marked by an evolution from 'the politics of power to the politics of ability', in which the knowledge and expertise directly related to production would be the criteria for exercising authority and participating in industrial society.[19]

THE ACCOUNTABILITY OF NATIONAL CORPORATIONS

Before treating the issues raised by the international activities of the corporations it is important to note the problems posed for representative institutions by the national enterprises. It is now fashionable to refer to the 'crisis' of representation and accountability, although discussion has been perhaps too narrowly confined to 'the decline of parliaments'. There is general acknowledgement that a syndrome of such factors as the complexity of many economic issues, shortage of time in the legislature, and party discipline and loyalty have hampered effective parliamentary surveillance of the executive. While government initiatives in economic planning have tended to further expose the unreality of accountability to parliament, it can be argued that developments in group politics also challenge governments. It is to the large corporations that we refer when we

[17] Galbraith, op. cit., Chap. 6. For statements on the separation of ownership from control see A. Berle and G. Means, The Modern Corporation and Private Property, Harcourt Brace, New York, 1932, and J. Burnham, The Managerial Revolution, Indiana University Press, New York, 1941. For a contrary argument see R. Miliband, The State in Capitalist Society, Weidenfeld & Nicolson, London, 1969, Chap. 2, and for a thorough review of the differing evidence see Child, op. cit., Chap. 3.

[18] For this convergence see Galbraith, op. cit., p. 391; Clark Kerr, Industrialism and Industrial Man, Oxford University Press, Cambridge, Mass., 1960, and Alec Nove, The Soviet Economy, Allen & Unwin, London, 1969.

[19] G. Ionescu, 'Saint-Simon and the Politics of Industrial Societies', Government and Opposition, Vol. 8, No. 1, 1973. See also D. Bell, 'Notes on the Post Industrial Society', The Public Interest, No. 6, Chicago, 1966.

suggest that the industrial system is imposing its values on society, making its goals those of the state, and thereby threatening to assume 'the substratum of sovereignty'.[20]

Some of the problems may be appreciated by briefly noting the relations between corporate and representative institutions in differing contexts. Very relevant here is the contemporary trend to a more emphatic style of corporate politics—in which decisions emerge from the discussions of group spokesmen and bureaucrats, and parliament is presented with *faits accomplis*—a return to a 'neo-feudalist' style of politics.[21] It is interesting to see how the guidelines for recent prices and incomes controls in the USA and in Britain have been drawn up with only perfunctory attention to the legislatures and how new sites of functional representation (Pay Board, Prices and Incomes Board, etc.) have been established. Some West European states, more committed to economic planning, have institutionalized the new group politics in functional chambers (such as the French Social and Economic Council) outside the elected assemblies. In the Netherlands the Council is able to make decisions for industry[22] and in Norway there exists a two-tier system of decision-making, the corporate-organizational and the electoral;[23] outside parliament the cabinet meets with labour, business, and farming lobbies in boards to bargain over economic policy.

But the sectional focus of the groups makes their activities difficult to reconcile with the national mandates of governments. In Britain, observers have been impressed by the role of the state as merely *primus inter pares* in the group politics; government is buffeted by and dependent on the groups for administrative co-operation and information.[24] Beer has persuasively related the convergence in

---

[20] W. Friedman, *Law in a Changing Society*, Penguin, London, 1972, p. 321.

[21] See Henry W. Ehrman, 'Interest Groups and the Bureaucracy in Western Democracies', in M. Dogan and Richard Rose, eds., *European Politics: A Reader*, Macmillan, London, 1971. See also David Apter, 'The Premise of Parliamentary Planning', *Government and Opposition*, Vol. 8, No. 1, 1973, pp. 3–33.

[22] See Stephen G. Cohen, *Modern Capitalist Planning: French Model*, Weidenfeld & Nicolson, London, 1969, and J. E. S. Hayward, *Private Interests and Public Policy*, Longmans, London, 1966.

[23] Stein Rokkan, 'Norway: Numerical Democracy and Corporate Pluralism', in R. A. Dahl, *Political Opposition in Western Democracies*, Yale University Press, New Haven, 1966.

[24] Shonfield, *Modern Capitalism*, particularly pp. 389 ff. For an important discussion on the British control of different types of corporatism see Nigel Harris, *Competition and the Corporate Society*, Methuen, London, 1972. Harris

policies between the conservative and labour governments to the common pressures of the great producer groups, regardless of the party in office.[25] The continuity of policy, regardless of party and the apparent 'imperatives' of planning in an industrial society, clearly seems to delimit the scope of influence of the policy choices of political parties and diminish the impact of the voter's electoral choice on the policy outputs.

Various measures of public ownership represent attempts to exercise some form of external political control. In Britain the basic industries such as coal, railways, gas, and electricity have been nationalized. Control has been vested in public corporations which are directed by an administrative board, not by the minister; the minister is responsible to parliament for broad policy but not day-to-day administration. This format was designed to achieve a balance between the objectives of public accountability and commercial freedom. However, public accountability in the British context hinges on two features: (a) the actual influence of the minister over the corporation, and (b) parliament's influence on the minister. As David Coombes and others have shown, both of these conditions are poorly met,[26] though this failure needs to be linked with the broader issue of the general breakdown of accountability. The lack of personal control by the minister is common to most large-scale enterprises, and the lack of effective ministerial accountability is related to the shortage of parliamentary time, the general weakness of parliamentary control of government expenditure, and the party loyalty of backbenchers to the minister. Ironically, ineffectiveness of public control has not improved commercial efficiency; the 'political' interventions by ministers and civil servants, who lack business skills, hinders the development of corporations as efficient businesses. Moreover, attempts to liberate businesses from governments, *via* state-holding companies, regulatory commissions, or government contracting have not satisfactorily reconciled the goals of commercial independence and public accountability.

---

draws a useful distinction between *étatiste* and *pluralist* versions; in the former the state is dominant, in the latter there is a bargaining relationship and groups tend to operate as self-regulating fiefdoms.

[25] S. H. Beer, *Modern British Politics*, Faber, London, 1969, pp. 318 ff. S. E. Finer, *Anonymous Empire*, Pall Mall Press, London, 1958, and Richard Rose, 'The Variability of Party Government', *Political Studies*, Vol. XVII, 1969.

[26] David Coombes, *State Enterprise*, Allen & Unwin, London, 1972, and W. A. Robson, *Nationalised Industry and Public Ownership*, Allen & Unwin, London, 1962.

The Italian holding companies, ENI and IRI, have enabled the state to purchase shares in many sectors and firms while stopping short of outright nationalization. It is clear that the enterprises have managed to exploit their commercial success for social and economic objectives, particularly for economic planning and post-war economic reconstruction. But in spite of formal provisions for supervision by the Minister of State Holdings, and parliamentary debate, public control is again weak.[27] The pyramidal structure of the group protects the constituent companies from day-to-day control; in practice the corporation is a mediator between government and parliament and the companies.[28]

In the United States it is often considered that the superior expertise of businesses has enabled them to take over the commissions originally set up to regulate them. The commissions are merely buffers between government and groups and the broad and vague delegations of authority to private groups help to buttress and legitimize a clientelist style of politics; a situation which Lowi has termed a form of 'interest-group liberalism'.[29] The well-known American bias against the assertion of state action prevents more thorough-going public intervention and the commissioners operate more as symbols of control.

A final expedient has been the contract device. In the United States much of the defence and space programme has been 'hived-off' to private groups such as universities, research groups and industrial firms. Similarly, in Britain, there has been an impressive growth of quasi non-governmental organizations which are in receipt of public funds but are not government departments. This has been a preferred method of exploiting the skills and motives of private enterprise for public purposes and, at the same time, avoiding the interference of government bureaucracy. However, the autonomy of the corporation is often gained at the cost of public accountability.[30] Representative institutions and governments have been ineffective in sur-

[27] For a thorough discussion of the Italian enterprises and the theory and practice of accountability see Stuart Holland, ed., *The State as Entrepreneur*, Weidenfeld & Nicolson, London, 1972.

[28] For the confidence of the technostructure that it knows what is in the public interest, see the remarks of Nigel Despicht in Holland, ed., *op. cit.*

[29] Theodore J. Lowi, 'Interest Group Liberalism', *American Political Science Review*, Vol. LXI, 1967.

[30] For an excellent discussion of the various aspects of accountability in this sphere, see Bruce L. R. Smith and D. C. Hague, etc., *The Dilemma of Accountability in Modern Government*, Macmillan, London, 1971.

veying contracted expenditure. This has been most notable in the defence, aero-space and engineering sectors, where the complex nature of the product or service often makes it difficult for the government to lay down guidelines in advance.

We would conclude, therefore, that in the industrial society there is a diffusion of decision-making outside the formal government, that accountability of corporations to representative institutions is often weak, and that it is increasingly difficult to separate public from private interests. Yet in the search for a new set of criteria, which will better define the public interest, government must beware of 'extending its reach so far that the concept of "private" loses all meaning or, conversely, of enfeebling itself through the diffusion of power'.[31]

THE ACCOUNTABILITY OF THE MULTINATIONAL COMPANIES

Many of these problems of accountability are now posed internationally. Developments in transport and telecommunications have annihilated the constraints of time and space, so helping the internationalization of economies and the integration and centralization of business. The linkage to advanced forms of technology may be the most distinctive feature of the growth of the multinationals. The multinationals are largely found in sectors where the products are homogeneous, mass-produced, and require high R & D costs. Petroleum, automobiles, and chemicals are examples of such products.[32] A major source of tension between corporations and states, therefore, stems from the corporations' concentration in sectors which are crucial for broad national economic planning or national defence. For most observers it is the speed with which the international corporations are integrating sectors of the economy across states that is most significant. There is the notorious projection from current trends that, by 1985, some 300 corporations will control three-quarters of the manufacturing assets in the West. Such grounded predictions, allied to the general trends towards internationalization and the interdependence of countries in several

[31] Bruce L. R. Smith, *op. cit.*, p. 55.
[32] Of the *Fortune* 500 large industrial enterprises, Raymond Vernon found that 187 were multinational, i.e. they had subsidiaries in six or more countries. He also found that in terms of numbers of employees, sales and plants in the USA, and profitability and R & D expenditure, these multinationals scored higher than the remainder of the 500. See *Sovereignty at Bay*, pp. 8–9.

spheres, form the background to Kindleberger's claim that 'the state is through as an economic unit' or to Vernon's assessment that 'economic sovereignty [is] at bay'. There are several illustrations of how this globalization of business has added constraints to, or weakened governmental control of, national economies.

First, by differential or transfer pricing across states, companies are able to escape national fiscal controls, not least in the full payment of taxes. Research has shown how the low degree of reported profitability among Swiss-owned firms in Britain is almost certainly the result of such financial switching; revenues were transferred from Britain to the Swiss parent, not as dividends from profits but as non-taxable royalty payments.[33] Second, states become too dependent for capital on the investment plans of large corporations. This was seen in 1968, when earlier US government guidelines and exhortations to corporations for the repatriation of capital, and limitations on the exports of investment were transformed into mandatory controls. American efforts to safeguard their balances produced hostile reactions in countries such as Belgium, Canada and Australia, which are heavily dependent on such investment.[34] The co-operation of the multinational companies with the rules underlined just how 'American' their identities and loyalties remained in cases of inter-governmental disagreements, and dramatically illustrated the vulnerability of host countries when the US government placed a global interpretation on its national interest. Third, there is the prospect that subsidiaries will be vehicles for the policies of the state in which ownership is incorporated. The most controversial applications of extra-territoriality have been made by the US government, in its attempts to supervise the overseas activities of US based corporations. The US government has indirectly dictated the sales policies of the affiliates of US owned firms in the light of its foreign policy aims and regardless of the policy aims of the government acting as host to the subsidiary.[35] The American computer industry and its subsidiaries were prohibited for two years from sup-

[33] Brooke and Remmer, *The Strategy of the Multinational Enterprise*, Longman, London, 1970.

[34] Cf. Jack Behrman, *National Interests and the Multinational Enterprise*, Prentice-Hall, New Jersey, 1970, Chap. 8.

[35] US refusal to allow the subsidiaries in NATO countries to export to the communist bloc has mainly applied to high technology products such as computers and radar. These extra-territorial applications are based on the US *Trading with the Enemy Act* and *The Exports Control Act*.

plying France with the computer capability regarded by the French armed forces as essential for France's nuclear defence policy. Exports to communist states of products wholly manufactured or even containing components made by American-owned subsidiaries in Canada, Britain, and France were also vetoed by the US Commerce Department in the late 1960s. Restrictions on the independence of the host-state are clear-cut here and arise from the influence of US government policy on the parent company, and on the foreign state, *via* the subsidiaries. Fourth, there is the element of uncertainty. It is paradoxical that at a time when governments are increasingly committed to promoting a wide array of social welfare and economic goals, often by means of planning, they are more and more constrained by the international environment. As we have pointed out, the subsidiaries of foreign-owned companies are often located in sectors which are central to economic growth, technology or exports, or even all three, while the traditional instruments for managing the national economy, such as tariffs, currency rates, monetary policy and so on are less effective.[36] Finally, by switching about their enormous sums of capital between different units of the enterprise, the corporations are able to undermine the strength of a country's currency.[37] This tidal wave of international liquid funds or 'hot money' (exceeding the total money supplies of Japan or Britain) is exempt from national controls, undermines a government's demand management policies and fuels inflation.[38] Moreover, the development of the Eurodollar (an international capital market, which is free from national control) enables the parent or affiliate companies to evade a government's credit restrictions. The development of the Eurodollar and Eurobond currencies are clear signs that the needs of international business have outgrown the national banking systems.

It is important, however, to distinguish the actual from the potential capacities of the multinationals and most of these threats are potential. The majority of corporations, most of the time, act as

---

[36] On the prospect of Europe's technological dependence on America see J. J. Servan-Schreiber, *The American Challenge*, Penguin, London, 1967. See also Jack Behrman, *op. cit.*, p. 63.

[37] The policies of corporations in scheduling the timing of payments between affiliate and parent companies, in anticipation of the British currency revaluation, were actually instrumental in precipitating the devaluation of the pound in 1967. See *Fortune*, 15 September 1968.

[38] Charles Levinson, *Capital, Inflation and the Multinationals*, Allen & Unwin, London, 1971.

'good corporate citizens'. It is easy to overlook this point because much of the writing on foreign direct investment has laid too much stress on the tensions between the multinationals and states.[39] Both parties, aware of potential gains as well as losses, are more cautious and ambivalent. Apart from the extra-territorial applications by the parent state there are few incursions on the legal sovereignty of states, though in practice there are constraints on management and control of the currency. Corporations are capable of exercising self-restraint and respecting the sensitivities of governments. ITT may be something of an exception in this respect. Even this company, however, by its massive bungling and incompetence, has proved to be a feeble giant. Its Chilean assets have been expropriated without compensation and the damaging US Congressional investigations have shown that states can exact information in appropriate circumstances where they have the will.[40]

The root cause of tensions between states and corporations may be less tangible and more psychological than the evasion of national controls and challenges to the formal sovereignty or authority of the government. The international corporations, by definition, possess a flexibility and a range of options not available to states and trade unions, and there is the unpredictability and uncertainty stemming from the vulnerability of the subsidiary to 'outsider' decisions. There have been examples and research to support these fears. Studies suggest that American companies tend to maintain central control of financial policies and wish to concentrate R & D in the USA. In some cases centralization has been carried to a point where local management loses autonomy and any local identity.[41] National economic controls seem less and less effective in the international society. In some West European states the fear of dependence on the United States has produced a cultural reaction, which has united in a curious anti-American alliance the extremes of the political left and right,[42] as well as more positive proposals for a European 'response'.

---

[39] Hugh Stephenson, *op. cit.*

[40] See Anthony Sampson, *The Sovereign State*, Hodder & Stoughton, London, 1973.

[41] Cf. Robert J. Alsegg, *op. cit.*, On the close control of French subsidiaries by American companies see Allen W. Johnstone, *United States Direct Investment in France*, MIT Press, Massachusetts, 1965.

[42] Cf. J. J. Servan-Schreiber, *op. cit.* For a sensitive discussion of these problems see Vernon, *op. cit.*, Chap. 6.

TOWARDS PEACE?

Any assessment of the specific implications of the rise of the multi-national corporation for world peace depends on the kind of scenario one has sketched regarding the pattern of state – corporation relationships. This question and the related issue of sovereignty also give rise to the value judgements of what is a good society. Many would welcome the erosion of sovereignty in the expectation that it would help to weaken nationalism and somehow to eliminate the myriad conflicting or non-complementary claims and aspirations of states which are seen as threats to peace. Some defenders of the multinational companies claim that their activities, by demonstrating the general ineffectiveness of nation-states as governing units and the irrelevance of territorial boundaries, will pave the way for more supranational institutions. Others argue that peace is better defended by strengthening the states and the loyalty of citizens to them. Four points are worth brief mention in this connection.

First, the gap between rich and poor nations seems bound to widen in the near future, not least because of the economic gains of advanced technology in industrial states and the pressure of population growth in less developed states on an already inadequate resource-base. The activity of the multinationals may actually exacerbate these trends because they encourage the industrial societies to increase their trade with each other while the third world's share of international trade is actually diminishing. This is not to deny the claims of the corporations to have boosted world aggregate output and trade, disbursed capital investment to receiving states and been the main agent for the diffusion of technological knowledge and research skills across frontiers. However, it is a reasonable guess that, unless the benefits associated with advanced technology and the internationalization of capital are more widely diffused, the tensions and frustrations within the countries accommodating two-thirds of the world population will threaten peace. The major problem, which the corporations alone (and, one hastens to add, the existing pattern of states) are unable to tackle, is less to increase world aggregate output than to achieve a more equitable distribution of wealth between and within states.

Second, it is important to acknowledge the other primarily non-economic threats to peace; these centre on historical grievances, national and regional loyalties and conflicts of ideology. Many writings on the corporations, whether they assume a hostile or an indulgent stance, invariably attribute great causal independence to the technological-cum-economic forces; there is an implicit assumption that the political institutions, ideologies and even the organization of the state will be moulded in line with the economic substructures. This has been most true of the 'post nation-state' analyses which see the corporations as catalysts for a more international order.[43] We would suggest that one needs to take a less deterministic, less reductionist view and to be sensitive to the importance of non-economic factors and the role of choice in determining outcomes. It is clear from the historical record that improvements in economic welfare do not necessarily assuage the sense of individual or group grievances on the economic, or, indeed, on other dimensions. In spite of the many converging features of industrial systems across states there is still ample evidence of the wide variations produced by such imponderables as history, political culture, and political leadership propensities regarding the role of the corporations and enterprises.[44] Japan has allowed foreign investment only under very strict controls while Canada had belatedly realized the costs of the massive penetration by US capital of her economy.

Third, and disregarding for the present any development of a more coherent set of intergovernmental or supranational institutions, there seems to be little clear-cut evidence for asserting that the globalization of business and the interpenetration of the interests of companies of different states either will or will not promote greater mutual understanding between peoples. Some writers analogize from the literature showing that cross-cutting loyalties and contacts make individuals more tolerant, and that individuals who are isolated from contrasting views tend to support extremist politics.

---

[43] The following three quotations illustrate the assumption that states will and should give way to the needs of the multinationals: (a) '. . . erosion of the rigid concept of national sovereignty, is a process that should, I think, be consciously encouraged' and 'For the explosion of business beyond national borders will tend to create needs and pressures that can help alter political structures to fit the requirements of modern man far more adequately than the present crazy quilt of small nation-states', George Bull, former US Under-Secretary of State, cited in Behrman, *op. cit.*, p. 182. (b) 'Business is in the vanguard of an economic one-worldism which is finding governments still pursuing their parochial sovereign interests', Barber, *op. cit.*, p. 234. (c) Corporate managers 'are creating a different dimension of economic truth which must sooner or later be reflected in the political mechanism to deal with it', Rolfe and Damm, eds., *op. cit.*, p. 34.

[44] Cf. Shonfield, *Modern Capitalism* and Vernon, *Beyond Sovereignty*. For a statement of the 'convergence' thesis see Galbraith, *op. cit.*, p. 391.

Ergo, interdependence and contacts between states will promote tolerance and larger perspectives. But there is equally impressive research which shows that where groups lack shared values – or what Karl Deutsch termed a common social fabric – contacts between them are stressful and threaten peace. The jingoistic reaction in several states to US domination of national industries indicates how such contacts may be interpreted as signs of dependence on and penetration of American culture, and resented as such.[45] The recent example of ITT's attempts in Chile to undermine a freely elected government on the grounds that it was unfriendly to business has been a case of transnational interests harming interstate relations. Threats of expropriation and their actual implementation and the claims of conflicting jurisdictions will also increase interstate tensions. As long as two-thirds of the giant multinationals (with turnovers in excess of $1 billion) are US owned and the top management of these enterprises is largely American, the popular belief that the corporations may, albeit unwittingly, act as agents for the international hegemony of the U.S. will be sustained. The large corporations need to be multinationalized in other areas than the location of their direct investment.

Finally, let us assume that the asymmetry between international corporations and national governments and trade unions is remedied and that the trade unions are organized for multinational bargaining and, say, the EEC is the precursor of future regional blocs of states. The question then arises: how attractive is a life in which corporate, labour and democratic Leviathans confront each other? Unless there are effective measures for decentralizing decision-making and implementing some democratic control, might there not be an increase in those negative qualities which critics have linked to the 'organizational revolution' and the consequent remoteness of decisions from those affected? The new forms of technostructural participation, recognized by Galbraith and others, still leave broader questions of accountability untouched. The process of technological advance and economic growth embodies a series of gains and costs which should be amenable to public choice. A major reason for the ambiguous response of many national leaderships to foreign capital is their awareness of the mix of economic gains and political losses entailed in the process. As one perplexed Canadian, aware of the benefits and

---

[45] Cf. Vernon, *op. cit.*, p. 249. It is interesting to consider the implications of the titles of some popular books: *The American Challenge* (France), *The Silent Surrender* (Canada), *The American Takeover of Britain*.

disadvantages of American investment, confessed: 'How do you compare apples and oranges?'[46] Establishing trade-offs between the two is bedevilled by the difficulty of quantifying the latter in comparison to the former. We are faced here with an acute case of the contradictory imperatives involved in the aspirations for economic efficiency and democracy. The former emphasizes virtues of large scale, deference to expertise, division of labour and centralization of decision-making; the latter emphasizes smaller units and the values of accountability, widespread participation and decentralization.[47] Ultimately, preferences about future arrangements depend on whether one applies national or international criteria to the idea of the 'public interest'. Is it co-extensive with the interest of the majority of the members of a state or with that of its government, or does it lie with the population regardless of states or regional blocs?[48] Some defenders of the corporations have come close to asserting that they know what is best for citizens regardless of popular preferences or government-stated programmes, and proponents of more federal or international institutions suggest that welfare needs will be best satisfied without the constraints of national borders.

Establishing a balance between the ethics of democracy and economic efficiency may best be achieved by relating the size of units to the nature of the function. The nation-states are too small for some purposes, yet too large for others. States may have to form federations to contain the multinationals, for example, yet they may have to decentralize much decision-making to regions, to achieve accountability and promote meaningful participation.[49] Alternatively, there is the socialist vision which rejects the choice, posed by Servan-Schreiber and the technocratic politicians, according to which the individual West European states face the alternative of

[46] Cited in Sidney Rolfe, ed., *The Multinational Corporation in the World Economy*, Praeger, New York, 1970, p. 26, or in the words of Mr Harold Wilson in 1966, when he was British Prime Minister, American investment would be welcomed for its expertise and technological benefits but 'capital investment in Europe [should not] involve domination or, in the last resort, subjugation'.

[47] For discussion of the relationship between size of organization and the worth of participation see Robert Dahl, *After the Revolution*.

[48] For the confusion surrounding the concept of public interest see Joseph Frankel, *National Interest*, Macmillan, London, 1971, pp. 40–3, and Chap. 9.

[49] Cf. Dahl, *After the Revolution*. For similar prescriptions applied to Western Europe, see John Pinder in R. Mayne, ed., *Europe Tomorrow*, Fontana, London, 1972, and Denis de Rougemont, 'Vers une fédération des régions', in *Bulletin de la Culture*, No. 2, 1968.

unilaterally submitting to an American-dominated capitalist Leviathan or combining to form a European one. For writers like Barratt-Brown, Miliband and Mandel the internationalization of capitalism offers not a choice between European and American versions of corporate capitalism but demands international measures of public ownership to make it subject to democratic control.[50]

IN CONCLUSION

At several points we have seen that the capacity, particularly of small and medium-sized states, to make independent policy decisions has been eroded by the activities of corporations. We have tried to suggest some of the strains industrial societies pose for the nation-state, including the centrifugal demands from within and the centripetal pressures from without. Both nationally and internationally corporations have been tending to escape the control of the institutions designed to achieve accountability. The authority of the central government is challenged internally by the decisions of these groups and externally by the international reach of the corporation. It is difficult, however, to establish precise links between, on the one hand, international corporate growth and, on the other, the erosion of the independence of states or the formation of regional blocs. The trends are accurately seen as responses to general changes in the international environment, advanced technology, the internationalization of production, and the organizational revolution.[51] It would also be unwise to exaggerate the degree of independence states have possessed in the very recent past at least, and delimitations of the autonomy of states have also been apparent in many non-economic spheres. In retrospect, the major significance of the mature corporations may well have been to emphasize the case for promoting new forms of accountability within states and for developing supranational or inter-governmental responses to the socio-economic

[50] See Miliband, *The State in Capitalist Society*, Weidenfeld & Nicolson, London, 1969, Mandel, *Europe versus America*, New Left Books, London, 1970, and Michael Barratt-Brown, *From Labourism to Socialism*, Spokesman Books, London, 1973.
[51] This theme of the reciprocal influences between, on the one hand, political and economic unity and, on the other, trends towards unification of the EEC states and the growth in transnational relationships between groups in the different states, emerges strongly in Andrew Shonfield's Reith Lectures, *Europe, Unknown Destination*, 1972.

internationalization. But I suspect that the more viable nation-states, however penetrated their economies, are likely to survive for quite a time yet. There are few signs that states are prepared to forgo the economic benefits of foreign investment or to give way to global or regional decisions on issues they deem vital. The 'state of nature' arising from the multinational enterprise problem will have to become much more unpleasant for the states to institute a new compact.

David E. Apter

The Premise of Parliamentary Planning*

THE TEST OF A THEORY IS IN ITS APPLICATION. THE DIFFICULTY IS that in political theory, application is rarely a sufficient test. This is especially true of the kind of theory in which I am interested. It is abstract, highly generalized, and for this reason, tends to be illustrated by means of applications which neither prove nor disprove. A lack of clear guides for disproof is one of the more serious deficiencies of highly general theory. If that is so, what is the point of doing it? One answer is that if such theory can lead in an *a priori* way to logically inferred predicaments which repeat themselves in many forms in the real world, this should allow us to anticipate events. This, in turn, allows us to compare these common predicaments in diverse settings to discover the necessary and separate it from the contingent. This can represent a big step forward if it results in new types of data and different forms of linkages between variables. The 'tests' then are more insightful generalizations rather than 'validations'. If such generalizations can be made subject to quantitative proof, so much the better. In any case, the route to validation is bound to be indirect. Propositions locked into a logical structure of thought will remain for long cumbersome and wearisome. Despite this, as long as not too many people waste their time with it, a general theory approach seems worth the effort.

A difficulty is that the effort required is very great and the results are not everyone's cup of tea. Moreover, the further one goes in this direction, the more austere the requirements of knowledge, empirical and abstract, qualitative and quantitative. At every stage the judgement about which variables to retain and which to throw out in a general scheme are subject to tough criteria: the logical integrity of the theory itself, and the difference it makes in the analysis of concrete conditions. Progress is bound to be slow. There are many

* This article was originally presented as part of a lecture series at St. Antony's College, Oxford in the spring of 1972, when I was Rhodes Visiting Lecturer.

trials, experiments in the mind, applications to problems of the day. Situations and events are surrogates of more extensive research which serves as a testing ground, not proof.

A STRUCTURAL THEORY

One such effort is offered here for more general discussion. I have applied certain principles of the theory of political choice adumbrated in various articles and developed in relatively parsimonious form in the first chapter of a recent book, *Choice and the Politics of Allocation*.[1]

In that book, I outlined a structural theory which juxtaposes two concrete units, society and government, with two analytical ones, norms (or political beliefs) and structures (or ways in which roles are allocated). There is continuous change at both levels, a redefinition of the meaning of norms which involves changing concepts of equity. Structures and the allocation of roles alter too. They do so not in response to changing principles of equity alone but according to functional needs of the productive system. Hence structures change according to function, norms change according to shifts in belief about equity. The resulting disjunction forms a field of information on the basis of which political systems act. Some use coercion, which in turn reduces the field of information. Others rely primarily on the utilization of some part or all the field of information. This in turn depends largely on the type of political system which prevails. The greater the participation, the more likely the system is to act on more information and the more information there is available.

This brings up several problems. When the functional allocation of roles and the principles of equity at the societal level show too great a discrepancy it means concretely that there is too much inequity according to the principles prevailing in the society. That means that some roles are receiving minimal rewards because their contributions are not functionally required or are even unnecessary for the on-going productive system. Such roles become *marginal* in functional terms. In a highly participant society, holders of such roles ought to be able to organize to make information about their predicament available, and back that up with votes. But there is a prob-

---

[1] For fuller statements, see my forthcoming collection of essays, *Political Change*, Frank Cass, London. The main theory is in D. E. Apter, *Choice and the Politics of Allocation*, Yale University Press, New Haven and London, 1971.

lem here. Marginals are weak, difficult to organize, and may be blamed for their predicament by the majority. For example, the almost universal equity principle of equal opportunity may only intensify the problem because it makes the marginals responsible for the condition they are in.

Another problem with systems operating on the basis of information is information glut. There is too much information. Processing is difficult. Knowledge is ambiguous. Government policy suffers as it tries to deal with functional complexity plus equity gaps. As development occurs and societies become more complex, marginality and information glut become tandem problems.

Can democracies arrive at new methods of maximizing information, of processing it, and above all of applying it to the condition of marginals? That is the question we want to discuss. It is built into the original theory. Our first hypothesis for empirical analysis is that marginals want a greater share in the equity of the system. This we call a tendency towards embourgeoisement. Their need is more access to roles. In turn this requires re-allocation. Meanwhile, normative disenchantment occurs in the more functionally significant parts of the society. Lack of equity causes alienation or, to put it crudely, a radicalization among certain sectors of the middle class, especially those most relevant for the creation and utilization of information for government. Hence the information creators show a radicalization from above, while there is a tendency among the marginals towards embourgeoisement from the bottom. They may sound radical – but rarely do they want to change the allocation system. They want fairer shares. Those at the top, increasingly concerned with immobility and inequity of allocation move to the left. Embourgeoisement from below and radicalization from above is the result.

The problem is how to create a better democratic political framework and how to allow these principles to be discharged in a manner benefiting the entire society. How to induce greater flexibility in role allocation becomes a singularly difficult policy problem for any government concerned with the condition of marginals. Private property, vested interests, local groupings, primordial wants, all these tend to immobilize governments. In turn, radicalization, if not rendered constructive, chews up bright and responsible people, forcing them to work at cross purposes, a condition wasteful of effort and costly in talent. Can a democracy meet the complex of demands, normative and functional without which it cannot sustain itself? The general answer is yes. But improvements are not easily forthcoming, especially if the normative and structural boundaries, the need for maximum participation, increasing political freedom, public control without bureaucracy and maximizing three types of information, populist, interest, and technical are to be respected.

In addition to these we make one other assumption. Political change always involves new forms of consciousness, concern for a political future, indeed a greater awareness of the need for structural change among significant sectors of the population. For this reason, radicalization, far from increasing alienation, may mean a new lease of life for parliamentary government. Parliamentary reform becomes interesting if we break out of the conventional mould of simple correspondence between class, interest and party. In turn we need to reconstitute the ingredients of a polity in order to seize a direction and promote new modes of work, education and models of political participation. To place government in a more intimate relationship to development, for example, means that in no way can it be described as mere super-structure. It breaks down the conventional distinction between society and political system, civil structure and state structure.

MARGINALITY AS SOCIAL COST

We begin our discussion with the proposition that the distribution of choices must always be made more equitable and must also remain scaled to human proportions. Choices are illusory if people are victimized by them or unable to utilize them, and dangerous if they are manifestly incapable of directing them.

The antique and privileged basis of parliamentary government is that it embodies the collective rationality for a society. It is the expression of public consciousness. Our assumption is that by planning, this rationality can be improved and the criterion is more equitable distribution. The mode of planning we have in mind is to be structured through the better use of high information.

The point of departure is the relation of marginality to representation. Marginality represents a claim against the society, a particular need which the satisfaction of other needs in the system does not abate. The problem is to transform the needs of marginals into a continuous re-definition of functionality itself. This inevitably leads to the rejection of the purely autonomous and self-legitimizing character of the way power is distributed. The question is how best to incorporate this in the structure of democratic government.

One answer is participatory planning of a sort useful to marginals as well as the rest of society. The total range of skills and knowledge which development produces needs to be maximized first on behalf of those with the greatest need. Marginality is the *social* cost of development. For each new increase in functionally significant roles there is a corresponding cost in marginalization. Participatory planning must reduce that cost through appropriate policies. By drawing attention to the plight of marginals we set a standard for a government enabling it to plan a more effective policy. This diverts the priority from development *per se* to its human costs.

This problem of priorities constitutes a tense and more or less permanent disagreement between those who urge the radical redefinition of society and those who cater to the complex needs of a highly developed social system. Such tension is aggravated in the growth of diverse and increasingly aggressive political sub-cultures. Competition intensifies within this sub-culture between groups anxious to discover what injustice has been done and those preoccupied with future developmental needs, particularly technical ones. As a result, the issues are continuously re-defined. They take on fresh meaning. And there is no simple correspondence between functional position and ideological views. For example, a radicalized bourgeoisie may articulate its own alienation and ventilate a nostalgia of alternatives. Today this expresses itself in a desire for greater rationality in politics. Some, the most radical, see that rationality becoming more possible once the condition of the marginals defines social cost and forms the basis for evaluating the whole of society.

With such a criterion as the object of political development, the next step is programmatic. It is to develop a polity which concerns itself with compensatory demarginalization, in the context of information utilization and low coercion or participatory planning. Needed for this is a method which renders the corporate structure of social life more congenial to human purposes within a democratic framework. This can be called a new form of a democratic 'reconciliation' system combining pluralism, planning, bargaining and representation.

PARLIAMENTARY CONTROL

The first and most important feature characteristic of participatory planning is its structure. Assume the framework of a representative and parliamentary structure but a renovated work load. Specifically, what we have in mind is a version of what has been referred to as 'indicative planning'. Indicative planning is a system of planning which relies on pointing out desirable ends rather than on giving orders to achieve them.[2] To make this effective requires methods of control beyond simple voluntarism. These become readily available when indicative planning is combined with socialism. But what sort of socialism? What seems the necessary correlate of parliamentary planning is what can be called 'commanding heights' socialism, i.e. where critical and important industrial enterprises (and relevant technical and research centres) can be strongly influenced and/or controlled by government through fiscal policy and other measures establishing priority. However, the organization of such enterprises, if they are not to become excessively bureaucratic, needs to be mixed so that joint public and private ownership can combine with relatively decentralized administration.

But not too much socialism. We want to retain the flow of economic information which arises from the market: we simply add new players, mixed enterprises. Government becomes a more serious market contender but not a controlling contender except in exceptional circumstances. By this means a parliamentary frame is placed around the economic market maximizing three types of information which now become freely available to government: *populist*, i.e. dealing with both the general welfare and the needs of real and incipient marginals; *interest*, dealing with the enterprises, special interest corporate groups and the needs of relative marginals; *professional*, maximizing technical information of all sorts. The problem is to find a reasonable political structure which combines control and information in a system of high obligation to the marginals while expanding choice in the society at large.

It should be clear then that we see participatory planning as based on a market within which information is exchanged. Populist and interest information is especially manifested in the needs of real and incipient marginals, which becomes a definition of what needs to be done. Professional information becomes the means of doing it. Government renders the needs into policy, using its power appropriately.

It is our contention that indicative planning, commanding heights socialism, mixed enterprise and decentralized administration, and a political market-place allow us to combine information with planning. However, these ingredients can hardly be put together in

[2] See Andrew Shonfield, *Modern Capitalism: The Changing Balance of Public and Private Power*, Oxford University Press, London, 1965, p. 84.

a mechanical fashion. If we learn nothing else from the study of political development it is that no set of political 'servo-mechanisms' work in anticipated ways. We are dealing with human institutions in all their complexities. Innumerable examples exist of commanding heights socialism turned into a bureaucratic nightmare, mixed enterprises and decentralized planning as excuses for corruption and tyranny and planning which results in monumental errors with the public left holding an empty purse.[3]

OPENNESS AND POLITICAL ELITES

Also required is openness at the base. However this does not necessarily mean a pyramid of administration in which cadres consult at all levels from local villages or communities to the top whether regional (based on population centres), ethnic (based on various racial or cultural differences), or functional forms (based on occupational clusters) which may produce paralysis. Cultural and ethnic representation based on primordial loyalty may be too separatist and parochial. Regional organization may be more useful at earlier rather than later stages of development. Functional organization, although becoming more and more significant, smacks of fascism or corporatism. The danger in a shift in emphasis to rational planning is that it may serve to shut out valid claims and feelings, the reactions to which can be swift and powerful taking the form of ethnic, tribal, linguistic, or religious conflicts (as occurred in Northern Ireland between Catholics and Protestants, Yugoslavia with Serbs and Croatians, tribal conflict in Nigeria or Basque nationalism in Spain).

Openness at the base cannot mean direct democracy. To organize information and translate it into messages is essentially the function of various elites. Political elites exist for the sole purpose of intervening between people in general and those who rule. Only in a society in which face to face relations are possible, a city state for example, can eliteness and citizenship combine, i.e. the number of elites being virtually coterminous with the society as a whole. In a very complex society the political elites are proportionately small.

Nor is the radical demand to convert the polity into small scale units or break it up into more manageable political bodies in a direct democracy, although a laudable object, likely. It is already necessary

[3] See Michael Ellman, 'Lessons of the Soviet Economic Reform', in *The Socialist Register*, Ralph Millband and John Saville (eds.), Merlin Press, London, 1968, pp. 23–54.

to co-ordinate the activities of too many diverse decentralized bodies. Some breaking up of large scale units into smaller ones, whether these are corporate firms, political units or societies, can usefully occur. But this will also magnify the problem in many ways and generate a need for new cadres of elites whose professional skills are appropriate to new forms of information gathering. Such elites create new corporate structures, a condition which is likely to worsen (with corporateness occurring in all aspects of life). It is already the dominant form of social organization. The question is whether such corporateness will overwhelm, swamp, or destroy the individual or allow him diversity, choice and efficacity.

Let us now rephrase the issue in the following terms. The totality of information in any system is a function of its openness. The *more open a system at the base*, the *more diverse its forms of participation*, the *larger the proportion of elites required to deal with an increasing pressure of information*. Assuming that the growing complexity and scale of large organization is not (realistically) going to be diminished by decentralization (because this introduces proliferation and new and complex forms of integration), how can openness at the bottom be organized and converted into rationality at the top? Rationality at the top is for us the urgent necessity – the political development task. Openness plus rationality are the twin ingredients we look for as the minimal requirements of a democratic system of planning.

With these difficulties in mind, let us turn to the political structure. The key to planning is the integration of types of information into a ranking of priorities on the twin basis of present needs or short term criteria, and future or projective criteria. Required too is an anticipatory sense of predicaments likely to follow any policy.

The most successful methods of planning have primarily occurred in countries engaged in the catch-up process. This is because the pattern which political leaders wish to emulate can be observed in more advanced countries and errors can be compensated for by coercion. Emulative planning only works of course when there is an example to follow. In a non-coercive, highly developed politics there are few working examples.

On the other hand, because there are too many unresolved difficulties facing highly complex democracies today, parliaments have become ritualized. Political action is in committees, behind the scenes. Indeed, it is surprising that people retain much faith in the legislative system at all except for a lack of better alternatives. It is a negative rather than a positive attachment. Terms such as 'parliamentary control over the executive', 'checks and balances', 'judicial review' and the other phrases originally intended to reconcile openness with rationality through the representative system are today simply clichés. Democracy is more and more a method, a bargaining process in which clusters of legislators make their pay-offs and calculate immediate gains and losses. Governmental policy is an odds figuring affair, with the result that the entire principle of democratic government is turned on its head. It is the game which counts and becomes its own purpose, with public policy its by-product. In an earlier period the situation was reversed. What counted more was improvement in public policy brought about by means of the recognition of newly relevant publics through the expansion of the franchise. Changing the rules of eligibility meant re-defining the public by including hitherto excluded groups. Today this form of pluralist and liberal coalition politics works only for those for whom it works.

The range of contemporary needs and the possibility of acting on the basis of long-range projections is more and more problematical. Planning is more suspect. The search for an appropriate concept of planning in terms I have described is really a test of how predictions can be made in social life. The conception of planning we have in mind is based on the organization of information into messages by different kinds of elites for the purpose of short term and long term planning. What is needed is a method of review built into the process at every stage. Hence our argument is to be seen as a return to first principles.

PARLIAMENTS AS PUBLIC PLANNING BODIES

Our solution is that parliaments should become forums of open debate on planning, participate in priority setting through legislative decision-making, and serve as agents of popular and technical review and revision. Party platforms would serve as programmatic schedules. A party programme would become a project, a statement of plans to organize policy issues. Governments would be elected on the basis of such proposals. One problem is how to make such proposals into serious statements of government intent. Another is how to expand the quality of expertise in both party planning and government planning. Today's technocrats tend to have little know-ledge of the character of political needs. Purely technocratic solutions are bound to fail. The planning process needs to go beyond narrow professionalism, with technical concerns translated into new forms about which the press can comment and people take sides. In short, planning requires an alliance between politicians and experts to create projects jointly for public evaluation.

Such parliamentary planning would rely heavily on the use of the mass media. Debates, voting on issues, and most of all the presentation of alternative priorities, require publicity. Television can be, after all, a most powerful instrument of primary political communication. It is not, however. As employed in the political process today it is primarily a campaign device. Politicians are viewed as salesmen, selling themselves to the public. In short, the public sees the politician primarily in his populist role. It rarely sees him take a stand or put his views forcefully in debate. Although an interested public is potentially vast, nothing is deadlier than debates as they are now. What could be duller than a day at the Congress or a day at Parliament (screened on unedited television)? The fault is not with the public or the media. Debates are dull because they fail to reflect the real substance of politics. The vitalization of the legislative system itself is needed in the form of parliamentary planning.

We suggest a government elected on the basis of planning projects, and capable of organizing and putting into effect programmes jointly devised by politicians and experts. Considerable controls over various corporate sectors would be required, necessary for indicative planning and commanding heights socialism.

The concept of parliamentary planning has as its object the organization of various kinds of information into priorities as follows: *general concerns affecting the whole society*; *specific programmes affecting interest*; and *variable compensatory programmes*. General priority concerns include broad policy objectives which define the public interest such as consumer sector development, educational reform, provision of research or technical facilities, etc. Such general concerns in effect constitute the broad overall objectives or programme on which a government stands for election to public office.

With more specific programmes, and here we have in mind the actual working out of the priorities in concrete terms (the who gets what, when, and how, of politics), a variety of ordinary programmatic legislation would need to be fitted into the more general concerns. Great flexibility would clearly be necessary at this stage, including balancing the functional needs and demands of specific interest groups. Since it is through such specific demands that general matters of public interest take concrete form, the result affects tax reform, fiscal policy, social welfare, cost of foreign assistance, etc.

The third category, compensatory variable programmes, is the most *ad hoc*, arising as a result of local demands, emergencies, protection, the need for rectifying errors, responding to changes in public concerns, etc. These include the most immediate, short term and particular.

General, specific and variable programmes all demonstrate somewhat different political characteristics. If the general constitutes a plan of government on which basis it appeals to voters, translating that into a concrete programme suggests a legislative format in which the populist and interest and professional information can be used as a basis for legislative differentiation. The first two are based on political estimates of what constitutes the public interest which in turn is a definition of what people want or need as consumers or citizens generally, as members of particular groups, occupational, recreational, in particular, and as marginals. What we envisage is a popular lower house with general priority, specific interest and compensatory variable programmes organized around populist and interest information and a professional upper house organized around integrated technical programmes, including overall fiscal and economic programmes, the predicted effects of one specialized programme (say housing) on another (say education), the objective being to force experts to put together, in a visible and appropriate way, the various specialities which each of them might otherwise simply pursue independently, often to the detriment of the whole.

It will be recognized that this notion of the legislative process as a method of planning combines general priorities leading a formalized, planned conception of the public interest, an overall project of fixed programmes, and specific or variable programmes which become tailored to the needs of the moment. Planning is thus a complex continuous process combining long term technical considerations and medium and short term reactions and demands.

As with any legislative process, most of its preparatory work would be undertaken in committees. Moreover, this would not be open to public scrutiny at this stage. No method of planning can be undertaken in the full glare of publicity at all stages. Flexibility requires sufficient privacy to enable legislators to change their minds. The public arena and the debates within it could afford publicity only as the result of a previous consultative process. As well, if governments were too vulnerable to loss of confidence and too easily overthrown, their ability to combine political and expert knowledge in the form of long-term and short-term planning would be seriously impaired.

Periodic elections at fixed intervals would be preferable. Elections would become significant as public referenda on planning as well as providing methods of putting officials into public office. However, if, as suggested, the government should not be politically vulnerable to being overturned during the planning period, the government's official life should be the same as its planning period. Near the end of its life, compensatory variable programmes would serve as a continuous amendment process.

Management of the ensuing debates would take the form of presented alternatives, each constituting a carefully worked out and prepared programme of options. Such options ought not to be cut and pasted together in public. Our emphasis on legislative planning requires careful consideration through prior consultation, selection, and rational evaluation in order to offer a serious and significant set of choices to the public and their legislators. Legislative decision-making would thus go far beyond the present patterns.

A NEW PARLIAMENTARY CYCLE

Since debate would precede the determination of programmatic choices, once a general legislative programme had been decided on, a government would be bound to carry it out. To prevent too much rigidity, however, the legislative process would need to shift gears and go into a second phase, changing its emphasis from deciding between programmes to reportage and from reportage to introducing modifications, i.e. the alteration of both specific and variable programmes. Hence the 'managed' phase of legislative decision-making in priority planning would give way to the critical revising and amending phase. As the legislative emphasis alters, a stable parliamentary cycle appears. Let us explore some of the implications of this cycle.

The role of the parliamentary party would certainly change with the rotation of the cycle. But, what is to sustain party discipline? We have eliminated the vote of confidence in favour of a fixed term of office. One answer is the work-load itself. Parliamentary parties would suddenly have more work of a purposeful nature than ever before. On the government side the parliamentary party would serve as the essential link between the party in general and the cabinet. Its tasks expanding at every stage, programme preparation, the presentation of alternatives to parliament, it becomes more professionalized. Indeed, the entire party mechanism takes on new functions, and joins with the party executive to think through alternative programmes.

At the same time, however, grounds for party affiliation would become more ideological. How much commanding heights socialism? What form of indicative planning? What major priorities and on whose behalf? All these are crucial questions about the future. Furthermore, any continuous testing of one's sense of the future requires not only a willingness to impose one's intelligence on it, but also the need to correct, without losing the essential purpose of the objects. Some of the usual methods, the threat of crossing the floor, or ordinary opposition during the course of planning debates would serve to sustain party discipline as they do now. Moreover, since a parliamentary party would go through its most severe trials at early stages of the legislative process rather than the end, as at present, solidarity at the point of maximum ideological debate could be crucial.

Party discipline thus relates to legislative rhythm. General programmes would take shape during the first year of a government's life. The more specific ones would follow. The variable programmes would become more significant towards the end of a five-year cycle, in the effort to patch up or compensate for programmatic weakness or failures. Party discipline would need to be strongest at the beginning of the cycle as the government party formulates its main set of alternatives and when the opposition could be expected to react most strongly. Crossing the floor would be most significant at just this point, i.e. where parliamentary party members offended most by any agreed schedule would want to join the opposition. In short, the need for maximum solidarity balanced by serious switching would seem most likely at the beginning of the cycle. More ordinary party discipline could be enforced subsequently, when ideological matters became less significant and more ordinary issue-bargaining the rule.

The activity of the parliamentary party would also change as the legislative cycle wore on, resulting from the need to serve as a corrective for the errors in original conception and scope of priority planning and the need to make provision for specific interests affected.

The object of the opposition parties would be to assess the costs of a government programme. It too would change as the parliamentary cycle moved on. Its original critique would be directed against the government plans overall. Marginals would have a direct interest in supporting opposition parties, especially as the legislative cycle wore on, in order to protect themselves if they could not obtain specific advantages and safeguards from government. Incipient marginals, by withholding support, changing allegiance, and organizing a base in the trade unions or in interest groups, would be concerned to direct government attention to their condition, while the real marginals would become the direct obligation of the society inasmuch as they represent the real cost of government planning.

The cycle, itself, implies first basic planning, then compensatory revision. The role of parliamentary parties would vary from projection of priorities to critical evaluation. Finally, evaluation directs attention to the costs of such programmes, particularly the human costs as measured by the condition of marginals, the latter becoming more significant as the cost of government programmes manifests itself in human terms.

The cycle is directly related to how information is used. The volume of populist interest, and professional information would increase as the cycle completed itself and the time for a general election approached. Since each party would need to have its proposal for priority planning organized prior to the election, all would need to be concerned to review the planning period well before the elections. To do this effectively would, in turn, require parties to decentralize, to ramify their organizations, and to reach out to lower levels in order to gain a more accurate sense of public need and public want. As they did so they would, in effect, organize precisely those groups which under the present system are likely not to be represented, i.e. the real marginals as well as engaging the better organized incipient marginals, trade unionists, various interest groups, etc.

Because of the need to establish projective programmes, parties would also be required to train their own cadres of experts on whom they could call to interpret, correct, inform, bringing politician and expert more closely together in party work and helping to provide experts with political and legislative experience.

So far we have had in mind domestic rather than foreign programmes. There is no difference between them in principle. Questions of security, overseas assistance, and diplomacy may require a greater degree of initial flexibility however. It is difficult to 'plan' foreign policy as one would development. But some planning is possible. For example, in the matter of overseas assistance, the US programme represented a major post-war reconstruction commitment to Europe and a much more half-hearted and uneven commitment to the so-called Third World. Sometimes in and sometimes out of phase with broad definitions of American national security, it has never been the subject of national debate or organized review. The public as a whole has never had a chance to ventilate its views on the matter intelligently. Nor have those with some expert knowledge in the field received much more than short shrift unless their views coincided with those of the government.[4] Nowhere is the need for rational planning on a visible priority basis more necessary than in the area of overseas assistance. The need is especially urgent to bring expert opinion into the public arena. Contingencies of foreign policy are necessarily very great, but if variable programmes (including secret and diplomatic and other arrangements) could be brought into a better relationship to the larger policy context, the whole picture might make much more sense.

Such parliamentary planning requires two houses, a method of resolution between them, an increase in parliamentary party discipline, an expansion in the significance of the party, a more intelligent critical capacity on the part of the media, and the arousing of more direct public interest. These are the variables. We can not here spell out actual mechanics (which would need to fit the cultural traditions, history, and particularities of each society concerned), but it is possible to suggest considerations which, much discussed in the literature, are appropriate subjects for a contemporary political theory. These are (a) greater and more constructive power by government over critical centres of social and economic life, checked by (b) more safeguards to individual liberty through an elaborated system of administrative and judicial reviews. It also implies that (c) the methods of such control should be subjected to decentralization and greater and greater degrees of popular participation in decision-making. We shall discuss several of these points more fully.

COMMANDING HEIGHTS SOCIALISM AND PUBLIC POWER

By commanding heights socialism we mean that the main corporate activities of a country should be vested in public or mixed public and private corporations or para-statal bodies. This extends the principles of government regulation several steps, without necessarily turning

---

[4] The effects at times have been tragic. In Viet-Nam, for example, the government 'listened' only to the experts it chose to hear and suppressed unpleasant information. See Daniel Ellsberg, *Papers on the War*, Simon and Schuster, New York, 1972.

such corporations directly into government-managed organizations. Included under this head are major corporations whose activities appreciably affect employment, wages and prices, defence and related industries, major national banks which render possible the more direct co-ordination of fiscal policies and government planning, and all major industrial enterprises which constitute 'natural and necessary combinations', joint-stock corporations, major holding companies and multi-product corporations. All these would properly come either under the commanding heights rule in the form of a para-statal corporation, or in the mixed private-public corporation.

The criterion is not size but how strategic an activity is in the life of the country. Moreover, to prevent ossification such para-statal bodies and mixed enterprises should compete with each other. Straight nationalization and responsibility for government operations, such as a national railway system, a national aviation system, ought not to preclude competition or drive out all economic competition from private firms. Indeed, government may own and operate such enterprises both in conjunction and in competition. Affecting their policies through subsidies and direct grants and other subventions, information about what to do derives from the market.

Of course, such para-statal bodies would need to conform to rules regulating corporate interests generally, operating under public boards composed of members of the various industries, consumers, trade unions, etc. But they would be subject to far greater degrees of participation in review or decision-making. We do not visualize direct worker participation in the management of such enterprises, however, unless – and this is a big exception – they are production bodies, i.e. actually turning out products.

This last brings us to an important point. The issue of worker participation in planning and running factories is not yet well understood. In principle a most socially desirable condition, worker participation bogs down in the sheer mechanics of participation. The time involved and the opportunities for manipulation, enlargement of trivia and related bureaucratic conflicts tend to result in high labour costs and inefficiency. Workers often feel hemmed in by responsibilities they may now need to share with management. In theory, worker participation in management is a good thing, but the practice may be questionable in output terms. At present it is very much subject to experimentation in Yugoslavia, Chile and elsewhere.

Worker participation offers new and promising possibilities and poses real difficulties. More and more it is being explored in conjunction with the elimination of assembly line techniques for certain products and the automation of basic construction methods, enabling firms to establish responsible work groups which share in the various stages of the process, from basic design to production. Not all types of production are susceptible to this kind of direct output responsibility, but something like this seems possible in a variety of industries. The more workers participate fully, the more they are responsible for the different stages of the production process.

Whether with worker-management or without it, however, mechanisms also need to be found to include broader public interests. Industrial boards need to act to set priorities; joining with representative bodies to elaborate industry-wide policy. Managers ought to be more free to take the necessary administrative measures to fulfil their roles, without interminable meetings and discussions.

REPRESENTATION OF INTERESTS

When we speak of parliament we mean an instrumentality by which information existing in society is translated into messages for the purpose of government and decision-making. We have already suggested a lower house organized around the translation of populist and interest demands, concerns, reactions, etc., into messages which require a response. This populist lower house, which would operate much as any legislative lower house works in most democratic countries, would include the representation of organized interests.

Attempts have been made to integrate interest representation with popular representation under guild socialism, and indeed under fascism. In our view, the range and diversity of interests plus their specificity gives to representatives of interests such unfair advantage over populist concerns that interest representation needs to be restricted by means of standing committees in the lower house. The rationale is as follows.

Whether private or public, the corporate bodies of a society need both scope and regulation. Given the complex world of contemporary enterprise and the rapidity with which change occurs, interest groups cluster under various functional categories such as business (including para-statal bodies and mixed enterprises), education, medicine, law and welfare.

To qualify for representation, interest groups would first need to be registered under the appropriate heads, on the basis of which the standing committees of the lower house would be organized. A particular enterprise with necessary qualifications would apply to the appropriate functional group for membership. In turn the functional group would select members to participate on standing committees in which roughly half the members would be representative of the lower house. If a new set of interests would seem to require a new functional category or head, need for such an organization would manifest itself first among interested parties. Application could then be made for registration and establishment of a new standing committee in parliament of which the primary purpose is to regularize the relations between interest groups and representatives of parliamentarians. Such a process may also be prompted by the need to promote competition between functional groupings on matters affecting all their interests, as well as instill more effective control over the legislative process of the lower house.

This emphasis on interest representation should not obscure the main role of the lower house as we conceive it. This house, popular in nature, would retain the conventional mode of constituency representation (with effective powers of amendment and veto of government policy). Interest representation, as we envisage it, would always remain subordinate to the populist part of the lower house, its proceedings made visible and identifiable to the public. It is to ensure a more regular control over interests and a recognition of their changing significance that we restrict such representation to functional standing committees.

However, the role of the lower house as a whole would change in its emphasis as the parliamentary cycle gained in momentum: from debate and approval of general priority programmes and enabling legislation, to specific reform bills, and finally, near the end of the cycle, the amendment of both in compensatory actions in response to public reactions. In this way the lower house would not only cement the relationship between governmental planning and public wants: it would have a more highly effective means for controlling the power of interest groups at critical stages of the policy-making process.

THE TECHNOCRATIC UPPER HOUSE

So far we have said very little about professional knowledge and what we have called a technocratic upper house. Such a separate upper house would establish a different set of mandates, although the objective, parliamentary planning, would remain the same in both houses. The upper house would be primarily concerned with long term or projective planning. Various priorities would derive from technical knowledge of social conditions.

Such a house is based on the assumption that the key feature of modern society is the generation of new information at increasingly rapid rates. This implies a new range of possibilities and priorities, the control of the development future – from the environment to the population explosion. However, the rationalization of technical specialities which would affect all people in society needs to be checked with short term interests. An upper house, consisting of technical specialists in planning, representing various research and technical bodies of a public nature, fiscal and economic, education and manpower, welfare and social services, security and justice, would be linked to various ministries. These, in turn, would share much of the responsibility for research on technical specialities and maximize the statistical and other factual data needed for making plans and projections.

Each of these groups would work separately in terms of their expertise at one level, in order to integrate their concerns in organizing long range plans and priorities. To be responsible for a plan requires technical people from each field to compromise, to accommodate their technical requirements to the needs of others in other fields.

Thus the two houses would be preoccupied with different aspects of the same phenomenon, planning in a public manner. Both would have opportunities for specialized consultation, one with interests and the other with specialists. However, parliamentary debate would require the integration of both types of plans, precisely the task of a cabinet. A cabinet, assisted by a resolutions committee, would be presented with alternative combinations of priority and plan arising out of consultation and parliamentary debate and which parliament would vote as a schedule. The cabinet would be free to amend, restructure, and alter such alternatives, to develop further or modify its programme. This in turn would need to be approved by the two houses sitting in joint session. Obviously such questions of how representatives would be appointed to the upper house would depend on a variety of factors, as would the question of whether both houses should have equal weight, veto powers over the other, etc., concerns that require discussion in terms of specific countries at specific levels of development and in the context of their separate cultural traditions and preferences.

Parliamentary and presidential systems as presently constituted are too often either organized systems of plunder, or they concentrate exclusively on the short run, leaving the future to take care of itself. This generates cynicism among participants and leaves most of the population listless and bored with parliamentary government. What is needed is a more ramified system of parliamentary planning which employs high information, which in turn requires a more effective party system, a massive use of the media during the legislative planning period, a reconciliation mechanism between short term popular and interest demands and long term projected needs. Elections on the basis of programmes which have projective value would stimulate interest in the political process which operates in a cycle or rhythm capable of dealing with two phases: first the 'project' phase, when a government offers its programmes for selection by parliament; and second a compensatory phase, when such programmes need to be adjusted, errors rectified and amendments made.

Participatory planning would thus require a populist lower house dealing with short term plans, interest and populist information, and the reactions of marginals, and a professional upper house to deal in the long term. To accomplish such purposes, a political term of five year intervals between elections is an appropriate one. It gives time for the integration of plans, and an evaluation of recurrent economic and political costs. The two houses would repair their conflicts in committees by producing alternative priority sets which would be decided in legislative debate. As the parliamentary cycle drew to a close, the errors and mistakes of the previous plans would help to form the substance of new and remedial planning, and the projection of new priorities. All this in the context of indicative planning and commanding heights socialism.

CONCLUSION

What we have tried to sketch out is a framework for greater participation at all levels in which more rational planning becomes possible than exists in most democratic countries, and where the varied experiences of France, the British parliamentary tradition, the open access of American interest groups, and the experience of worker participation can all be brought together in a new synthesis.

The presentation here has assumed that constitutional protection of fundamental rights would be assured in any democratic political system and that, indeed, this kind of planning mechanism would require a more elaborate system of protection for individuals and groups than presently prevails anywhere. Without going into the matter, it is clear that something like a French Council of State and its administrative courts, perhaps combined with the Swedish idea of an ombudsman, is more and more necessary. The more organized and rationalized life becomes on one level, the greater the need for individual protection on the other. Administrative courts alone cannot do the job. Protection afforded by the courts ought to be at public expense, since one of the grosser inequities imposed by the court system is the high cost of litigation and the time involved.

Finally, we have not said anything about the civil service. We assume, however, that over time the civil service will gradually become more and more specialized and 'technocratized'. In short, while the civil servants may not all be experts in the full sense of the term, they will require more specific knowledge, more specialized expertise. This, in turn, suggests that the old 'generalist' tradition of the civil servant, whose humanity is a function of his broad and possibly classical education (the Macaulay ideal) is a thing of the past. However, as we have pointed out in the early part of our discussion, the radicalization of the bourgeoisie extends to the tendency among highly educated and technically trained civil servants. Theirs is also a greater concern with what might be called the civilities, a sense of aesthetic knowledge, and a greater philosophical awareness. We do not suggest, of course, that this very civil civil servant is as yet very common. But the cult of specialization is already being compensated for by greater sophistication. A 'concerned civil service' is possible even among technocrats. And if our assumptions about the radicalization of the middle class are correct, then the outlook for such civility is promising.

There are, of course, many problems not touched on here. How to prevent a civil service from congealing and hardening in both its technical and ideological predispositions is one. The methods of recruitment, the need for retraining, refresher courses, and perhaps the use of specially designed postgraduate courses (super-grandes ecoles) might be considered. The point not to be lost sight of, however, is how to emphasize the human values of the society as a whole. Planning is a way to make those values visible in the form of official concern. The organization we have suggested is designed to make as coherent as possible the different needs and demands people might have in an increasingly complicated universe, with organized participation, on issues which are understandable, to raise the level of public criticism and debate, and render compatible those short term and long term concerns which define the essence of choice.

David Coombes

'Concertation' in the Nation-State and in the European Community

THE MAIN SUBJECT OF THIS PAPER IS THE PROCESS OF GOVERNMENT IN which the political institutions of the European Community are engaged. The question at issue is what that process of government is likely to contribute to the achievement of cohesion, order, and stability in the part of the world covered by its member states. The approach which is tested in this paper is to take the concept of 'concertation', as it can be derived from recent experience of economic policy-making and administration in West European states, to develop it into a general political concept describing a method of government, and then to apply it to describe the process of government which the Community's political institutions have developed. In this way we shall raise at a level of abstraction some personal doubts about the Community's process of government based partly on experience of 'economic concertation' in the nation-state and partly on the experience of decision-making in the Community itself. It will be left to the reader himself to judge how far these doubts affect the governability of the Community; in some ways the author's own inclination, following the intellectual exercise required by this paper, is to qualify the value of the concept of governability in relation to the European Community, and to draw attention to other criteria.

THE CONCEPT OF 'CONCERTATION'

It has not proved possible at this stage to carry out a thorough survey of existing literature on 'economic concertation' or on all possible applications of the term 'concertation'. For present purposes the concept is derived from the post-war experience of economic planning in France. In essence it expresses the 'spirit of the Plan', as described by Jean Monnet: 'an association of all the economic and social forces of the country in a common effort'.[1] However, 'concertation' has both political and economic overtones.

Politically it signifies a process of government in which the participation of the representatives of interest groups is seen as the chief means of legitimating decisions. More specifically it is a method of making the exercise of the power of government to manage the national economy more representative, by obliging government to consult the main 'economic forces' (that is, trade unions, large corporations – public and private – and other professional and social groups) before taking economic decisions. However, the process of consultation is also seen as a means whereby the power of government over the national economy can be extended. In this respect it has been emphasized that the effectiveness of French economic planning has not depended on legal powers of government, or for that matter on a process of legislation. The measures required have not been those which would normally pass before parliament (except probably when they involve budgetary measures). Thus 'concertation' may be said to give an extra arm to government to act in the public interest, over and above the powers which it has obtained already by means of ordinary legislation. Here lies an important principle: namely, that in a democratic society government must be prepared to act on the basis of the consent of those affected, even though it may be exercising power over them. The aim might be the same as that in a totalitarian state, that is to say, the achievement of certain collective social and economic goals, but the method is essentially different.

In economic terms 'concertation' may be said to have four important elements for us, although these have not necessarily all been present all the time in French economic planning. First, there is the idea that economic decisions taken within government itself should be co-ordinated in the light of some set of overall national economic objectives. Secondly, there is the assumption that overall national objectives can be stated in terms of a set of major options. Thirdly, there is an ethical content, based on general objections to profitability as a motive of business men and on a feeling that the individual

---

[1] Quoted in V. Lutz, *Central Planning for the Market Economy*, Longmans, London, 1969, p. 168.

objectives of corporations and groups should be set in terms of some general view of the common good. Finally, a form of public direction of the national economy is adopted which is intended to preserve individual freedom and de-centralization of economic decision-making by relying either on centralized forecasting without direct intervention, or on what have become known as 'soft' techniques of direct intervention (mainly consultation with those directly affected). Combination of these four elements is meant to provide the benefits of a state-directed economy without the disadvantages, political and economic, said to be associated with a collectivist economy containing extensive state ownership, centralization of decisions and so on.

This method of government prevails outside France in various forms. What has been special to the French experience has been the emphasis on indicative planning, with its main element of centralized forecasting; but the fundamental principle of extending the power of the central government in the national economy, while at the same time avoiding excessive centralization or disruption in the pattern of ownership, has been followed at some time or another in the post-war period in every member-state of the Community.

It should be stressed, therefore, that in this use of the concept, 'concertation', participation is not an end in itself.[2] The inclusion of representatives of interest groups in policy-making and administration by governments is a much wider and older practice than 'concertation'. What is particular to 'concertation' is the deliberate attempt to give those representatives the duty of authorizing, even of initiating, new forms of government activity which lay down general obligations in the public interest. Thus, although its application so far has been primarily economic, the concept has a crucial political meaning because it implies a distinct method of government.

This method of government has been fashioned for the attainment of certain general economic ends which are now widely accepted in Western Europe. These are the ends of the modern welfare state: national economic stability, reflected in continuous full employment combined with stable levels of prices; national economic growth, used to provide an increase in the standard of living; control of the secondary consequences of economic activity in order to maximize welfare; pursuit of egalitarian aims in the distribution of income.

[2] Compare the discussion of participation in B. L. R. Smith and D. C. Hague, eds., *The Dilemma of Accountability in Modern Government*, Macmillan, London, 1971, pp. 92–7.

These ends influence the conduct of all governments, provide important criteria by which all governments are judged by electorates, and provide the material of most political activity in the member states of the European Community.

The essence of 'concertation', as it is considered here, is that it is regarded as a method of attaining these ends on the basis of two important criteria: (1) that the activity of government should be based on a consensus of the affected economic interests (meaning in practice the representatives of trade unions, trade associations, corporations, firms, etc.); and (2) that the basic theoretical principles of a private enterprise economy should be observed, implying preponderance of private ownership of the means of production and maximum freedom of decision-makers in the market place.

POLITICAL PROBLEMS OF CONCERTATION IN THE NATION-STATE

It is impossible in the context of this paper to examine the effectiveness of 'concertation' from an economic point of view. In analysing the application of the concept in national experience we shall offer a political critique. The first two elements of this critique, however, draw on the economic meanings of the concept.

First, we shall make a rough empirical generalization that the pursuit of ends of the welfare state in most of the member states of the enlarged European Community has been continually frustrated in practice by short-term difficulties in managing national economies. These so-called 'short-term' difficulties may arise from persistent causes, but they arise in the form of unforeseen crises, threatening one or another of the ends of the welfare state, or – what amounts to the same thing – upsetting the balance of interests upon which 'concertation' is based. In British experience the most notorious example has been the impact of current balance of payments deficits and of currency speculation on domestic cyclical policy. Indeed, one might say in general that one of the main limitations of national economic policy is the existence of international trade and the inability of any national economy in the sort of countries of which we are speaking to insulate itself against the outside world. As we shall see in a moment, membership of the European Community, with the commitment to allow free movement of goods, labour, services, and capital increases this limitation dramatically.

The 'short-term difficulty' or 'crisis' may take a variety of forms, but experience suggests that no government can seriously pursue the economic ends now considered general without acquiring the means of surviving recurrent threats of this kind.

The real problem is that in most of the states which we are considering a balance among the different ends has to be maintained if 'concertation' is to be viable as a method of attaining them. For example, if growth could be adopted as an overriding priority then the task of government might be more simple.

Stability as an end is very much more difficult to combine with government by 'concertation'. Perhaps a reason for this, a reason which is very interesting from a political point of view, is that government by 'concertation' tends to force government too persistently and too intensely into the role of a referee, a role which interest groups do not wish to perform themselves. In other words the costs of tenure of power outweigh the benefits for any potential holder of office. In 'concertation' the opposition consists of a set of interest-group representatives none of whom seek to obtain power themselves, and, therefore, none of whom understand or accept the discipline of office. This is satisfactory, so long as there are goods available to satisfy the particular interests concerned. If all or most players have to lose, however, then the referee has a hard time.

Secondly, the logic of 'concertation' seems to be difficult to maintain in practice. To be effective centralized forecasting and allocation must threaten the individual freedom of economic actors. If the problem is not a technical or cognitive one in the age of computers, it remains a political one in that a true de-centralization of the power of decision (especially with regard to such questions as the sharing of markets) is not compatible with reliable projections centrally produced.

This problem can be illustrated in an interesting way by reference to the attempts by British governments to influence the decisions of public corporations responsible for nationalized industries in the interests of macro-economic policy, while at the same time relying on the principles of the market economy for assessing the performance of individual concerns.

All post-war British governments have emphasized that the boards of the nationalized industries are themselves responsible for the performance of their own undertakings and the main justification for this has been that the undertakings operate in competitive conditions and that the principles of management adopted within them should be the same principles as are adopted in most efficient private enterprises. Since the early 1960s the main criterion of performance adopted for individual nationalized undertakings has been a financial objective, expressed in terms of a return on net assets, and indicating an agreed rate of profitability for the concern. Interference with these criteria, however, has been frequent, whether arising from the needs of the government's macro-economic policy (calls for restraint in pricing and investment), or flowing from welfare policies of the government of the day (for example provision of uneconomic services in rural areas and employment of uneconomic productive factors). Frustration on the part of the directors and managers of the nationalized undertakings has been prevalent, and it has been impossible in effect to rely on criteria based on private-enterprise market principles while preserving the government's macro-economic objectives.

The alternative would be to abandon the existing criteria of performance and to regard the nationalized undertakings strictly as agents of the government's economic and social policy-makers. Reluctance to follow this alternative is partly a consequence of differences between government policy-makers themselves (often in the same ministry): some emphasizing the need for co-ordinated and socially-inspired strategies for transport, energy, steel production and the rest; others seeking to promote economic efficiency or to carry out their responsibilities as 'bankers' or 'shareholders' to these public undertakings (most of which borrow heavily from the public purse). Yet it would be difficult for any government to resolve this conflict, while the double ends, first, of co-operation and, secondly, of competition are being pursued at the same level and at the same time.

This same conflict is inherent in the method of 'concertation'. It is as if governments were intent on evading an important and politically charged decision, regarding what kind of authority and what kind of motivation should predominate in the production and distribution of certain goods and services. Governments feel somehow that they should take responsibility for these activities, but they dread the consequences of doing so, and prefer to leave the outcome to a combination of official persuasion and entrepreneurial guilt.

One way of easing the problem with publicly-owned industries might be to alter the terms of ownership, thus clarifying the purposes of the government's role towards the undertaking concerned. In the minds of directors of nationalized undertakings it seems that meaningful de-centralization implies freedom to draw up and

operate corporate objectives. In turn this means freedom to take
risks and to bargain over market shares, freedom to conduct labour
relations on the basis of the undertaking, freedom to diversify, and
the right to depart from competitive pricing in the interests of
corporate development. With respect to the last of the claims it is
worth noting that de-centralization of business management in
nationalized industries is seen as being hindered by the enforcement
of general rules of economic behaviour, such as marginal-cost
pricing, based on the assumption of perfect competition. In other
words the problem seems to be one of structures rather than one of
processes; one of politics rather than of econometrics.

As we have seen, it could be treated where nationalized industries
are concerned by treating these undertakings as extensions of the
normal public administration and by applying principles of organization based on hierarchical lines of command and observation of
general rules. No British government has ever dared to risk this
approach, however, and few students of management would maintain that such an approach would be feasible where the management
of large commercial and industrial undertakings was concerned.
For example two areas where entrepreneurial motivation seems to be
essential in practice are labour relations and development of new
technical processes. In the interests of effective exploitation and
management of industrial resources, therefore, the corporations
responsible for nationalized industries should be put on a par with
those responsible for private industries.[3]

However, experience of government-industry relations in the
private sector is comparable. For example the labour government's
experiment with adjudication of proposed price increases in the
private sector led to arguments that the government's concern with
limiting price increases could only be sustained if the government
were also concerned with profit margins, and therefore with the
internal efficiency of undertakings. At the end of its life that government and its agent, the National Board for Prices and Incomes,
were moving in the direction of a nationally organized system of
reviewing business objectives and commercial policies in the light of
firms' cost-price ratios. The consequences of such a tendency if
followed to its logical conclusions for the size and the quality of

---

[3] On the background to this problem and on possible solutions see my recent
study, *State Enterprise: Business or Politics?*, George Allen & Unwin for PEP,
London, 1971.

public administration are alarming. The implications for business management are no less radical. Under the present conservative government, 'concertation' has again broken down, but it has been replaced by crude regulation of prices and incomes regardless of economic efficiency.

Our point is that 'concertation' as a method has concealed a difficult choice about how economic activity should be conducted. In practice most governments have found it necessary – publicly or not – to make a choice, and in few of the states of the Community is 'concertation' still the predominant method of economic policy-making and administration. In France itself, it was probably never more than a screen behind which it was easier to preserve the tradition of paternalist and protectionist state intervention in spite of dramatic changes in industrial structures and managerial styles. In Britain and Italy in different ways attempts at indicative planning, at 'soft' intervention (in one by consultative commissions, in the other by state-owned corporations) and at achieving incomes policy by consensus (if attempted in Italy at all) have all concealed what has been in effect a free-for-all. In the Netherlands, budgetary policy again seems to be the determining element in political as well as economic success or failure. In Western Germany no one can seriously believe that economic prosperity has been achieved at the expense of a shift in the balance of decision-making power among groups or between groups and government. In conclusion, then, the second element of our critique leads us to doubt whether 'concertation' does represent a genuine alternative method of government at all.

Thirdly, even if it were a viable and logical alternative, we could still ask whether it would be acceptable from the point of view of representative government.

At this point we should focus on the purely political meaning of 'concertation' as a means of by-passing, or even of undermining, what we might call generally 'parliamentary' methods of government. Without going into a full analysis, it is enough to repeat that 'concertation' depends on the direct co-operation and approval of interest groups and ideally obviates the need for legislative and budgetary authority. Parliament may not be excluded, but it is certainly not necessary. In this respect we should be ready to confess partiality in criticizing 'concertation' from this point of view. To some, as to the supporters of the Fifth French Republic, this aspect of 'concertation' was of course one of its most endearing features, and the Gaullist regime seems to have tried to develop it into a theory of representation in its own right.

Without going so far and without becoming too anxious for parliamentary government we could maintain that 'concertation' is a way of extending the role of government into new spheres of political action, rather than one of replacing traditional means with others. However there are plenty of examples to show that the conflict with parliamentary government is unavoidable. 'Concertation' requires discipline, not only on the part of group representatives bargaining with government, but also on the part of government itself. This discipline can be at its most demanding where budgetary policy is concerned. However, since, in traditional democratic theory, most budgetary decision-making by governments is meant to depend on parliamentary approval, then there is a persistent danger that plans forming part of concerted deals will be vitiated by parliamentary obstruction. Alternatively, and this is more likely in practice, parliament is blackmailed into accepting proposals for public expenditure, either because governments have entered into commitments to powerful groups, or (again more likely) because conceding the demands of the groups places such constraints on macro-economic policy that public expenditure is the only flexible element.[4]

In conclusion, therefore, what alternatives or supplements to 'concertation' have been employed or recommended in the countries in which we are interested here? The recent history of industrial relations in Britain seems to be pointing towards the conclusion that methods of government, based on electoral and parliamentary support and relying on regulatory intervention, are far from indispensable in managing the economy, at least in inflationary circumstances. In the last resort a government which is faced with implacably hostile attitudes on the part of organized labour has no alternative but to resort to devices such as formal regulation backed by appeals to the electorate. Where the distribution of income is paramount, consensus among functionally representative bodies (such as trade unions and trade associations) may well disregard and even exacerbate forms of disequilibria such as regional imbalance, extremes of poverty and wealth, and so on. Secondary consequences

[4] In a symposium on the role of parliament in modern budgetary decisions, covering six West European countries, and edited by the author, it emerges that interest-group influence is one of the main reasons for the decline of parliament's power of the purse. (The symposium is to be published shortly by Political and Economic Planning.)

of economic activity, like pollution of the environment or disregard for amenity, tend not to enter on the agenda of the normal participants in 'economic concertation'. Both these problems and those of income distribution might well be better managed by regulatory powers and procedures, in which the government acts not so much as a referee among affected interests, but as a law-giver responsible for enforcing the general interest. Again, in so far as the purpose of management of the economy is seen to be ensuring a fair and efficient allocation of resources geographically, then an alternative to 'concertation', with its emphasis on centralized processes of decision-making, might be greater emphasis on regional power structures. Where the direction and management of business is thought to affect many different interests and so be in need of structural reform, then one solution might be wider representation at the level of the undertaking itself, through such measures as worker-participation, government appointed directors and so on.

In other words if we recall that the different ends of the welfare state are equally important, then we must say that 'concertation' certainly cannot be adopted as an exclusive method of economic government. And if we also remember that the viability of 'concertation' itself demands that those ends are pursued to a large extent in balance with each other, then we must doubt whether 'concertation' as a method is not subject to inner contradictions which gravely restrict its application in modern democratic countries. At the same time we have observed that conflict seems to be inevitable between 'concertation' and parliamentary government.

'CONCERTATION' AND THE PROBLEMS OF THE EUROPEAN COMMUNITY

In the first place, there can be no doubt that the Community is an attempt to deal on an international scale with the problems faced by 'concertation' in the nation-state. The economic ends of the welfare state are written into the Treaty of Rome; in other words, the establishment of the common market and the other measures provided in the Community treaties are adopted primarily in order to defend or achieve the objectives of stability, growth, welfare, and social equality. The treaties emphasize 'negative integration', that is to say the removal of barriers to trade, the free movement of labour, services and capital, and so on, so that the means adopted in the treaties for achieving these objectives are increasing competition in a larger market with various regulatory mechanisms. However, the member states themselves have now acknowledged that the Community cannot survive unless it takes a more positive approach.

The establishment of the common market has itself raised severe economic problems for the member states. First free trade threatens the stability of individual national economies. We noticed before that one of the major challenges to economic concertation in the member states was the threat of short-term crises in such external factors as the nation's balance of payments. Free trade within the Community exacerbates this problem by outlawing restrictions to intra-Community trade. At the same time the Community required the establishment of a common market in some areas where managed markets were the rule. Thus in agriculture and transport political rather than economic solutions have been sought. It is now well known in the Community that a common agricultural policy based on centrally-fixed prices cannot operate effectively without fixed exchange rates. Discoveries of this kind have led the member states to agree to seek to achieve an economic and monetary union, implying that the common system of decision-making and law should extend to cover the whole economic sphere. Some writers have gone so far as to maintain that without an economic union in this sense a common market is 'unviable', mainly through its effect on the policies for stability adopted by the governments of member states.[5]

John Pinder has already shown in a famous article how a high degree of 'positive integration' is required in order to provide stable policies dealing with the member states' balance of payments problems in a common market. He has also argued that the problems which have emerged so far are primarily structural, social and political.[6] Remedies such as centralization of decisions regarding exchange rates, competition policy, fixing of external tariffs, forms and rates of taxation, will not be equal to the task. His own remedies include such measures as public control of prices and incomes determined by market power wielded in circumstances of oligopolistic competition, active labour market policy to encourage mobility, greater political authority for regions, participation by employees in the direction and management of their firms.[7] These and other

[5] J. Pinder, 'Problems of European Integration', in G. Denton, ed., *Economic Integration in Europe*, Weidenfeld & Nicolson, London, 1969, p. 143.

[6] J. Pinder, *ibid*.

[7] J. Pinder in R. Mayne, ed., *Europe Tomorrow*, Royal Institute of International Affairs, London, 1972, pp. 268–88.

reforms which he proposes do not seem to require centralization or harmonization of procedures and practices, so much as: first, a strengthening of public authority as representative of the general will in society *vis-à-vis* group interests wielding market power; and, secondly, the introduction of structural and procedural reforms to produce a kind of vertical devolution of public and private power. Both sorts of remedy are different from 'concertation': the first because it emphasizes direct intervention by government, and the second, because it seeks to diffuse the power of decision-making rather than to centralize it.

If our analysis of 'concertation' in the nation state is correct, then we can certainly confirm this assessment of the challenge facing the European Community, as it attempts to develop into an economic union. Indeed, the experience of the Community itself so far has provided additional evidence of the inadequacies of 'concertation' as a method of government. The Community's political institutions have relied mainly on consultation with interest groups and with representatives of national governments for achieving co-operation and consensus in economic affairs, and have despised parliamentary methods, which might have presented a direct challange to the sovereignty of the member states and underlined the political aspects of the decisions which were involved. The methods which have been adopted, however, have not proved very successful[8] and are certainly inadequate for the challenges to come. Papers issuing from the Commission and the communiques from summit meetings of heads of state and government give some indication that the Community's decision-makers are well aware of this fact. So far, however, they seem to have little to propose in the way of concrete constitutional changes.[9] Indeed most emphasis so far seems to be placed on legalistic devices for strengthening the power of the European Parliament to object to legislative and budgetary proposals. To move in that direction, on the basis of some vague notion of legitimacy, would seem to be little response to the alleged need

[8] For a critique see my *Politics and Bureaucracy in the European Community*, Allen & Unwin for PEP, London, 1971.

[9] See, for example, the Commission's proposals for the second stage of economic and monetary union. There are throughout vague references to 'institutional weaknesses' and to the need for making the institutions more democratic (two legalistic measures for giving the European Parliament a greater say in decisions are proposed). The only mention of practical measures to strengthen executive power comes in 'three remarks' (p. 28) none of which involve substantial, or adequate, changes.

for effective intervention by central institutions. What would seem to be more appropriate, for the measures which the Commission now seems to envisage as necessary for the second stage of economic and monetary union, would be a strengthening of executive, not of parliamentary, power. The relationship between those two has not been carefully considered, either in the report of the so-called Vedel group [10] or elsewhere. [11]

On the other hand the failure of the Community to respond to external challenges in the currency field has illustrated that a monetary union cannot be managed where the unanimous assent of governmental representatives is necessary for decisions. However, to transfer powers of economic intervention from the national governments to the Community would be to settle those powers at a level where even parliamentary government does not exist. If in the member states parliament has been by-passed, or even undermined, by 'concertation', in the Community it has hardly ever existed. 'Concertation' in the Community is nevertheless threatening parliament in the member states by a familiar process in which the accountability of national governments to each other, in the framework of joint decision-making in the Council, impedes their accountability to national parliaments. However, if in fact the ends of the welfare state are to be sought through the common market, the governments will be obliged to establish Community organs of central direction and control in economic affairs and to provide, as techniques for these organs, common standards and principles of economic management and conduct. Thus the pluralism enjoyed by having national economies and polities will be lost without any compensation in terms of a federal democratic process.

'Concertation' has also proved inadequate for harmonizing legislation. For the Community has had great difficulty up to now in gaining acceptance by the member states of proposals for harmonizing differing national standards and practices. Yet there are few fields in the economic sector where the Community can intervene by general legislation without encroaching on national procedures and standards.

[10] Report of the *ad hoc* committee to examine the problem of increasing the powers of the European Parliament. Brussels, 25 March 1972.

[11] The European Community Institute for University Studies in Brussels is currently undertaking research, financed by the Thyssen Foundation, on problems of policy-making in the European Community. This deals with some of the crucial problems raised here. The results will be published in 1975.

In conclusion, therefore, one might see in the process of government exercised by the European Community's institutions something which gives the worst of both worlds. While, on the one hand, there is insufficient authority at the centre to respond to the threats to welfare created by the common market, on the other, there is an intensification of the remoteness of government and of the weakening of parliament. In one sense (the economic), the national governments are made weaker by their membership of the Community; in another (the political) they are made stronger at least *vis-à-vis* their own parliaments.

EPILOGUE

This conclusion might not seem so relevant to those who are alarmed by a threat to 'cohesion, order and stability'. On the other hand they are of course not the only or even the most interesting criteria by which a process of government might be judged. It is a great relief to be asked to judge the Community as a process of government (rather than as a process of integration), and to be incited to use the language of political ideas (rather than that of mechanical engineering or biology). One's only reservation in this paper has been that there are other political ideas than those of Thomas Hobbes.

As for 'concertation', there is no doubt that the concept is extremely valuable for describing what seems to have become the dominant method of making decisions in the community. Above all it evokes the peculiar attitude towards representation prevalent in the community institutions – one which eschews parliamentary and constitutional processes in favour of private, informal contacts among selected individuals. This is the attitude and this the method of decision-making which must be put to the test of analysis. Whether 'concertation' could be viable as a process of government remains to be seen. Again, there is much to be said in political science for borrowing terms from the practice of politics rather than from other sciences altogether. Nonetheless even in the inebriation of creative effort, the rules of scholarship still apply: compare like with like.

Geoffrey L. Goodwin

The Erosion of
External Sovereignty?[1]

'EXTERNAL SOVEREIGNTY' IS THE CONCERN OF THIS PAPER, AND THE extent to which it has been eroded, in substance if not in form, by the pressures of the modern world. The formal distinction between external sovereignty and internal sovereignty needs to be emphasized at the outset. Externally, sovereignty connotes equality of status *between* the states – the distinct and separate entities – which make up our international society. Internally, it connotes the exercise of supreme authority by those states within their individual territorial boundaries. From Bodin who, in *De La République* (1577), saw *souveraineté* as the exclusive right 'to give lawes unto all and everie one of its . . . subjects and to receive none from them' to the Permanent Court of International Justice which, in the Wimbledon Case (1922), held that the sovereign state 'is subject to no other state and has full and exclusive powers within its jurisdiction without prejudice to the limits set by applicable law', the concept of the sovereign state has implied both supremacy within and equality of status without.

This then is the formal position. 'Without a sovereign state's specific persuasion no other state or institution may exercise governmental functions within its boundaries, or speak or act on its behalf in external matters.'[2] Yet do we not need to draw a further distinction between the *status* of sovereignty in legal and diplomatic convention

---

[1] This is the slightly revised version of a paper presented at the IPSA World Congress held in August 1973, in Montreal. I am indebted to Dr Harry Gelber for some helpful comments on an earlier draft.

[2] Alan James, 'The Contemporary Relevance of National Sovereignty' in M. Liefer (ed.), *Constraints and Adjustments in British Foreign Policy*, Allen and Unwin, London, 1972, p. 18.

and the *capacity* to exercise that sovereignty effectively in day-to-day diplomatic life? The status of sovereignty implies recognition by other members of society that the sovereign state is not subordinate to any other state, and that in diplomatic and legal convention it should be accorded equality of treatment with other sovereign states, irrespective of its power. All sovereign states have certain rights – and duties – which derive from the fact of their sovereignty. Yet the *capacity* of a sovereign state to exercise these rights raises very different issues. Much of the later argument here will be concerned with the extent to which the capacity of states to exercise the rights that derive from their sovereignty has been so circumscribed by the increasing pressures of the modern world and by the growing inter-dependence and inter-penetration of states that in practice sovereignty itself has become something of an anachronism; or to put it another way, whether the capacity of states to order their own internal affairs and to conduct their own external policies has been so undermined or eroded as to make the concept of state sovereignty increasingly irrelevant in practice despite its persistence in legal and diplomatic convention.

Before turning to this central issue, however, a very brief look is desirable at the traditional recipes for reconciling the notion of the sovereignty of the state with that of international order, for if this were to prove impossible, then in a nuclear age the days of the sovereign state would indeed be numbered. In other words, just as within the state the sovereign has traditionally been seen as subject to certain restraints, so internationally the concept of the sovereignty of the state externally has to be reconciled with at least that minimal degree of order necessary to ensure mankind's survival. Two main recipes for such reconciliation can be discerned; the differences between the two are not, of course, as sharp as this very brief summary implies.

The first recipe which, for want of a better word, one might term the rationalist, has pretty consistently held that an international society of sovereign states is not necessarily one characterized by persistent anarchy or lawlessness – as the realist might hold – and that a system of international order analogous to that to be found in domestic society can be achieved without setting up some kind of common authority with power to enforce edicts on the rest of mankind – as the protagonists of world government or federation advocate. To the rationalist most states, like most men, both share certain basic moral and legal principles and recognize the need to respond to the 'general interest' of the community of nations. There is here the Lockean assumption that, as in domestic society, the majority can be counted upon to act together to maintain a peaceful and relatively just order because of the majority's sense of obligation to the community of nations as a whole. Despite its growing interdependence this community is as yet no more than a quasi *Gemeinschaft*. With the progressive integration of states and peoples it may yet burgeon into a true *Gemeinschaft* of the whole of mankind. In the foreseeable future, however, the sovereign members of the present international community will continue to be sovereign though interdependent; the hope is that as they come better to appreciate the implications of their interdependence they can be weaned away from their traditional bellicosity in favour of peaceful collaboration towards a world of 'Peace, Progress, and Justice'.[3] Despite the setbacks of the past twenty-five years, this kind of recipe still has many adherents, including some of those within the contemporary school of Peace Researchers.

To the realist the basic flaw in the rationalist approach is not, of course, their acceptance of the continuing durability of the sovereign state, but their assumption of the solidarity, or incipient solidarity, of a society made up of sovereign states. To the realist, international society is a *Gesellschaft*, not even a quasi *Gemeinschaft*. It is an exemplar of the Hobbesian predicament of mankind, that state of nature characterized by a 'perpetual and restless desire for power' and 'by that condition which is called war'. This condition of war is not necessarily one of overt conflict; it is a condition of incipient conflict arising out of the proximity of states within the same vicinity, of their competition for scarce resources, and from the lack of a common authority to impose order – to 'keep them all in awe'. Moreover, to suppose that growing interdependence necessarily makes for a more orderly world is a dangerous illusion. On the contrary, as Stanley Hoffman writes, 'It is one of Rousseau's deepest insights . . . that interdependence breeds not accommodation and harmony, but suspicion and incompatibility.'[4] In any case, to set against the increasing technological interdependence is the marked proliferation of sovereign states over the last twenty-five years with the break-up of West European empires, as well as the cultural fragmentation of international society with the resurgence of indigenous cultural systems and the persistent ideological fissures. In many respects

[3] The slogan of the United Nations General Assembly.
[4] S. Hoffman, *The State of War*, Praeger, New York, 1965, p. 62.

international society is now a more fragmented society and sovereign states, whether new or old, cannot be counted upon to show any great sense of community-mindedness. As in the past, their decisions are likely to rest mainly on calculations of where their own interests lie and the amount of power and influence they can muster to pursue them.

If the durability and egoism of the sovereign state is not to be denied, for the realist the main source of order in an international society of sovereign states is the exercise of countervailing power in such a way as to restrain and contain those who seek to use their power to threaten that order. 'If the state system of Europe is to exist', wrote Friedrich von Gentz, 'and be maintained by common exertions no one of its members must ever become so powerful as to be able to coerce all the rest together.' So it is by reducing the incidence of conflict and mitigating its destructive impact through a balance of power, checking and restraining the overweening ambitions of the powerful, that the realist has traditionally hoped to reconcile the centrality of the sovereignty of its members with the achievement of a modicum of order – and perhaps even of justice – in an international society in which they co-exist. In a nuclear age some of the dimensions of this recipe may have changed, particularly in the acceptance of the need for more sophisticated forms of crisis management, but the substance remains.

There are, nevertheless, those who challenge the view that the sovereign state is likely to persist into the foreseeable future as the basic unit of international society. The rest of this article will sketch in, and examine critically, the main lines of their argument. The first is that the restructuring of international society in a more distinctly hierarchical manner has given the hegemonic powers whether in the West, namely the United States within the context of NATO and the other alliance systems, or the Soviet Union in the East within the system of socialist states, a dominant voice in the organization of their respective spheres of responsibility to the point where other so-called sovereign states within these spheres are no longer truly sovereign; they may be nominally so, but practically they lack the capacity to exercise their sovereignty. NATO may, in Karl Deutsch's terms, constitute a 'pluralistic security community' rather than an integrated one, but for most of its life the United States has been the 'core' power around which the alliance system has been organized and the dependence of the other members of the system upon the American nuclear umbrella and a really substantial American military presence on the continent of Europe in effect, it is claimed, derogates from their sovereignty. In particular, within the integrated command system of the North Atlantic Treaty Organization it could well be argued, as President de Gaulle did once argue, that integration has more often than not turned out to be a euphemism for control. And control to such a degree that at times it so closely circumscribes the exercise of sovereignty by other members of the system as to deprive them of one of the central attributes of that sovereignty – i.e. non-subordination. Or at least this is how the argument runs. Yet the relative ease with which France was able to assert her sovereignty in 1966 and to withdraw from NATO (i.e. from the military side only, not from the Treaty) casts some doubt on the argument,[5] as do France's qualified success in developing her own 'independent' nuclear capability and West Germany's initiatives in the realm of *Ostpolitik*. This is a complicated issue, but most of the evidence suggests that NATO remains an exceptionally close-knit coalition of sovereign states rather than even an embryonic integrated community (as distinct from a pluralistic security community) transcending that sovereignty. Members of the coalition have voluntarily accepted limitations on their freedom of action for their mutual benefit – 'Hang together or hang separately'. But it is not to be assumed that the coalition will hold together indefinitely or that others may not follow France's lead. Consequently, in my view, coalition membership in the NATO context is an instance of the exercise of sovereignty, not of the erosion of sovereignty. Similarly, although the Organization of American States has at times been represented as little more than an instrumentality of Washington's hegemonic influence throughout the Western hemisphere, the picture generally in that hemisphere has been of its members exercising an increasingly independent voice and being able to do so relatively unharmed by the evident displeasure of their big neighbour. Even where the United States has sought to use the system to legitimize its interventionist policies, whether in Guatemala in 1954 or the Dominican Republic in 1965 or unsuccessfully in Cuba in 1961, it has had to make concessions in order to secure the necessary diplomatic backing. In the economic field also the Kennedy Administration's initiatives through the Alliance for Progress have shown the limited efficacy of economic inducements in bringing about changes in the

---

[5] Even if one allows for the extent to which France's special geographical position enabled her to avoid what might otherwise have been the strategic penalties of doing so.

economic and social structure of aid recipient countries. Above all, in South East Asia the limitations of power, even of a power as great as the United States, have been strikingly displayed. In other words, although a core power or a hegemonic power can exercise great influence and often severe pressure, it has yet to be shown that it can, short of the overt use of force, bring about a radical and really fundamental change in the constitutional autonomy of the target state; in other words, that it can deprive that target state of the most significant attributes of its sovereignty.

When one turns to the socialist state system, or to that part that is under Soviet influence, the picture is somewhat different. Apart from the inhibiting influence in Eastern Europe of the presence of the Red Army one reason is that in Marxist-Leninist doctrine the notion of national sovereignty is held to be a transitory notion and part of the bourgeois paraphernalia which has no room in a world in which the proletariat 'has no fatherland'. However valuable sovereignty may be as a shield for a socialist state which sees itself as the bastion of the socialist camp in an encircling hostile capitalist world, the concept of sovereignty is held to be subordinate to the building of socialism. In particular, in relations between socialist states, the notion of sovereignty is subordinate to the interests of the whole socialist commonwealth. The key-note here is that of the 'unity of the socialist camp', not national sovereignty; the ultimate reality at the level of doctrine is the class struggle, not the assertion of national identity. The doctrine of 'limited sovereignty' adumbrated after the occupation of Czechoslovakia in 1968 was a natural extension of this Marxist-Leninist doctrine, even though, in Brezhnev's words, it was an 'extraordinary step dictated by necessity'. This is doctrine, however. That the practice may diverge appreciably, if only temporarily, is suggested not only by Rumania's example but even by Brezhnev's description of the doctrine of 'limited sovereignty' in Belgrade (September 1971) as a 'fable' and by his assertion that the 'roads and methods of building socialism are a matter for the peoples . . . of the individual countries' (of the socialist commonwealth).[6] This may well turn out to be little more than a tactical retreat. Yet there is a good deal of evidence to indicate that the appurtenances and attributes of sovereignty are not only prized as highly as ever by other members of the socialist system but that the Soviet Union seems to be rather less reluctant than in the past to recognize their appeal.

[6] *The Times*, London, 23 September 1971.

It is, however, on the impact of the technochronic revolution – of the accelerating technological progress and of advances in particular in electronics – that most of the critics of national sovereignty seize. The argument is too well known to need much elaboration. Basically it is that modern technologies, electronics and communications systems, the spreading ethos of industrialization, and the spread of technologically sophisticated ways of waging war, are all eroding the technological, economic, and sociological base of national sovereignty. Moreover, the emergence of ecological, economic, and social problems on a global scale, for instance, the problems of pollution, of resource depletion, of the utilization of the resources of the ocean bed, are all problems which transcend national frontiers to the point where only a global approach is likely to prove effective. In short, the argument is not simply that interdependence is a spur to interstate co-operation but that an increasing number of problems of this kind, together with the range of pressures to which states are subject, are beginning to outstrip the capacity of the sovereign state to cope with them. The functionalist school, led by David Mitrany,[7] has argued, to put the matter very briefly, that these trends have led to the identification of a range of problems which are essentially of a 'technical' nature, the handling of which needs to be entrusted to international organizations whose limits of competence should be defined by the nature of the problems themselves rather than by the interests of the governments concerned. The hope is that a thickening web of technical agencies will make frontiers meaningless 'through the continuous development of common activities and interests across them'. The sovereign state is seen as an impediment to the rational management of these transnational activities which is essential for human welfare and the hope is that the developing habit or practice of co-operation on a technical and expert level will gradually overlay political differences, and even, in time, erode the sovereignty of the participating states. The neo-functionalists, such as Hass and Lindberg, would seem to go rather further and to envisage a process of integration in which states cease to be wholly sovereign and so mingle, merge, and mix with their neighbours as to lose the actual attributes of sovereignty. Haas does indeed look to a shift of loyalties, expectations, and activities leading to the emergence of new supranational centres of authority, and although Lindberg seems to accept the more modest goal of nations foregoing their

[7] See in particular, D. Mitrany, *A Working Peace System*, Quadrangle, Chicago, 1966.

autonomy of decision-making in order to arrive at collective decisions or joint decisions, he also does not exclude the possibility that they may eventually delegate the decision-making process to new central organs. Both envisage that in this process of integration political actors will be persuaded to shift their expectations and political loyalties to this new centre. In short, although the earlier functionalist challenge to the sovereign state was mainly to be seen in the context of welfare, the neo-functionalists seem to have a broader approach, envisaging the emergence of supranational authorities, albeit initially on a regional basis, which will replace the sovereign state as a prime focus of political loyalties and expectations. Both argue, however, that: 'The needs of the modern world are overtaking the state, depriving it, *de facto*, of its supremacy and separateness through the establishment of over-arching institutions.'[8]

John Burton also stresses the extent to which our conceptualization of society needs to be modified in response to the thickening web of transactions across state boundaries – the 'cobweb' model. The nation-state model with its emphasis on relations between states and their relevant power is for him to aggravate the problems of conflict and to perpetuate an out-moded model. In contrast, 'An image of world society that depicts transactions, controlled and regulated by local state and international authorities, with a view to securing the maximum benefits from interdependence without loss of security, leads reasonably to integrative policies.'[9] For him, the 'clue to our problem of altering the [sovereign] state basis of world society is not in universal functionalism alone, but in decentralized administration within states, combined with increasing centralization within world society of those functions, such as the control of standards and agreement on common procedures, which can serve commonly felt needs'.[10] Again, for him, this process will bring a shift in loyalties away from the nation-state and will lead eventually to the erosion of state sovereignty through the diminishing value which peoples will place on the state as an effective instrument for achieving their values and goals.

Yet the basic premises of these approaches are, to say the least,

[8] Alan James, *op. cit.*, p. 22. For a fuller examination of these schools see Paul Taylor, *International Cooperation*, Elek books, London, 1970.

[9] John Burton, *World Society*, Cambridge University Press, Cambridge, 1972, p. 45.

[10] *Ibid.*, p. 119. How decentralization internally is to be reconciled with centralization internationally is not explained.

controversial, even were one to ignore the steady political and cultural fragmentation of the world over the last fifty years or more. The technochronic revolution has indeed wrought great changes. Distances have lost much of their terror – and their charm; industrial 'know-how' and managerial skills are more easily transmitted (though not necessarily more readily implanted); and communication networks have created at least an illusion of interdependence. Psychologically, the world has in a real sense become a 'global village', tied together in an 'intimacy of conduct and interdependence of welfare and a mutuality of vulnerability'. Nevertheless, side by side with the pace of international integration *between* sovereign states there has been the process of integration going on *within* the sovereign states. 'National integration seems to be the dominant trend which refutes speculation since the Second World War concerning the obsolescence of the nation state.'[11] It could also be argued that this process of national integration has been accentuated by the extent to which the 'modern welfare and "modernizing" state ... is continuously strengthening its own psychological foundation in people's valuations and expectations'.[12] In short, the technochronic revolution may have accentuated a sense of interdependence *between* states, but this has been accompanied by an extension of state intervention, of state sovereignty, *within* the domestic realm which has also been reflected in the widening range of competencies which the state asserts in its external diplomatic relationships.

Nor is it altogether proven that the international society of sovereign states is becoming increasingly interdependent even in the economic realm. Foreign trade as a proportion of gross national product has shown little or no increase since the beginning of the century, whilst the mobility of one of the major factors of production, namely, labour, has appreciably decreased. Following the breakdown of the 1930s, the world economic system has achieved a considerable degree of liberalization over the last fifteen years or so, but there are many signs of a reversion, in the last few years, to what John Knapp has called 'reluctant Mercantilism',[13] of the intrusion of, for instance, trade issues into 'high foreign policy', an intrusion accentuated by the gradual decay of the 'rules of the game' enshrined in the Bretton Woods agreements and GATT which in the past twenty-five years

[11] Robert W. Cox, ed., *International Organization: World Politics*, Macmillan, London, 1969, p. 297.
[12] Gunnar Myrdal, *An International Economy*, Routledge, London, 1956, p. 35.
[13] John Knapp, 'The New Mercantilism' in *Lloyds Bank Review*, January, 1973.

enabled trade to be relegated to a 'low level' issue.[14] That a high degree of interdependence still exists, specially amongst the 'market economies', is not to be denied and the range of choice of many rich, industrialized and poor, commodity exporting countries is often closely circumscribed by this interdependence – though, of course, in different ways. Nevertheless, the world economy encompasses not only the relatively 'open' market economies, but also a great diversity of often semi-autarchic and politically oriented national economies in which political ends determine economic means more often than economic needs prescribe political forms. This is not a simple picture of the 'erosion' of sovereignty in an increasingly interdependent world.

Moreover, the argument that a thickening web of technical agencies will in itself render meaningless the sovereignty of the participating entities is a myth which surely by now should have been dispelled by the actual experience of the specialized agencies within the United Nations system. It is true that the more indispensable of these agencies (e.g. GATT or, in the past, the IMF) often limit the manner in which the member states can exercise their sovereignty in terms of the legal constraints they accept, in terms of the political choices they have to make, and occasionally in terms of the jurisdictional freedom they can exercise within the domestic domain. But the activities of the great majority of the specialized agencies in no way threaten the identity of the member states, nor do they derogate in a significant fashion from their decision-making capacity. On the contrary, it can be argued that by providing instruments of collaboration which have helped their member states to respond better to the demands of the external environment they are perpetuating and strengthening the sovereignty of those states rather than eroding or diminishing it. Nor is there any substantial evidence to support the hope that such institutions (most of which, after all, command very modest resources) can become the focus of the loyalties of the citizens of the member states. This could happen and may indeed be happening within the European Community, but it certainly is not happening at the international level.

[14] Richard M. Cooper, 'Trade Policy in Foreign Policy', in *Foreign Policy*, No. 9, Winter 1972–73. Also Fred C. Bergsten: 'The US actions of August 1971 signalled the final collapse of the post-war systems and the accelerating evolution towards controls and nationalist mercantilism continues to this day.' *The Future of the International Economic Order: An Agenda for Research*, The Brookings Institution, January 1973, p. 72.

In some ways a more interesting and sophisticated argument forecasting the demise of the territorial state was that of John H. Hertz
who argued in 1957 that whereas for centuries the characteristics of
the basic political unit, the nation-state, had been its 'territoriality',
that is, its relative impermeability to outside penetration and thus its
capacity to afford protection to its citizens, the means of destruction
available in a nuclear age may render defence nugatory by making
even the most powerful 'permeable'. Both he and others claimed that
the nuclear age 'seemed to presage the end of territoriality and of the
unit whose security had been based upon it'. In other words, it
seemed to portend the demise of the sovereign state. The argument
was from the start based on the rather odd assumption – odd at least
to 'continentalists' – that the 'permeability' of the state was a mid-
20th-century phenomenon. Alan James thus rightly points out that:
'What nuclear weapons have done . . . is not to undermine military
impermeability but, for most States, to underline their existing permeability.'[15] And it is precisely their 'mutual permeability' which is
both one of the stabilizing elements in the 'balance of deterrents'
between the nuclear giants and a more promising safeguard of their
national security than the only relative impermeability that any ABM
(antiballistic missile) system, however 'thick', could provide.

John Hertz has also more recently acknowledged that there are
'indicators pointing in another direction; not to "universalism" but
to retrenchment; not to interdependence but to a new self-sufficiency;
towards area not losing its impact, but regaining it; in short, trends
towards a new territoriality'[16] and a new territoriality which would
point to the durability and persistence of the sovereign state as the
basic unit of the international system. The reason for his second
thoughts are complex and cannot be given full justice here. Amongst
them, however, he instances the marked forbearance of both the
nuclear powers – the 'muscle-tied giants' – in their dealings with recalcitrant small neighbours. Whether the caution with which the
large resort to force has been partially responsible for the ease with
which the small have done so is a moot point. But the incidence of the
use of force by small or medium powers in the last decade certainly
does not suggest that they have been deprived of this prime attribute
of sovereignty. Nor does the ability of a Cuba or an Iceland to stand

[15] Alan James, *op. cit.*, p. 26.
[16] John H. Herz, 'The Territorial State Revisited: Reflections on the Future of
the Nation State', in James N. Rosenau, *International Politics and Foreign Policy*,
rev. ed., Free Press, New York, 1969.

up to the pressures of greater neighbours suggest that they see sovereignty as either nominal or irrelevant; better to be a Czecho-slovakia than a Belorussia, a Lesotho than a Namibia (South West Africa). Moreover, although many of the states that have become independent during the last two decades initially lacked any obvious national identity and had to operate within artificial frontiers set by the European colonial powers, recent years have seen the consolida-tion of these states within their boundaries, the growth of some kind of national identity, especially where the peoples concerned have had to fight long and doggedly for their independence, and a wide mea-sure of legitimacy accorded to their international personality. Whether or not the 'territorial imperative' will provide a firm base for the durability of these often rather fragile states must still be open to doubt, but it is quite possible, as John Hertz points out, that the process of modernization as it proceeds within them will both accord the state a greater organizational capacity and defence cap-ability and provide it with a legitimacy in terms of the needs of its citizens which at present it frequently lacks. Moreover, it could be argued that the 'on-going rush of mankind into the technological conformity of a synthetic planetary environment' makes the sover-eign state more important than ever as 'the custodian of cultural diversity' which has for long been one of its traditional justifica-tions.[17]

A slightly different approach is to be found in Andrew Scott's *Revolution in Statecraft* in which he points out that in this century formal government relations have been 'increasingly supplemented by informal relations, in which the agents or instruments of one country are able to reach inside the borders of another, with or with-out the knowledge or approval of the government of the second country'.[18] This growth of 'informal access' or 'informal penetra-tion' can operate at any number of different levels, the ideological, the economic, and the political (in terms of covert operations). And it is not necessarily the prerogative of the strong, witness the forms of penetration attempted by the United Arab Republic and by Cuba. This informal penetration may in a number of ways challenge a state's capacity to exercise its sovereignty effectively. For instance, movement of funds, persons, ideas, information, and material across national frontiers may be very difficult to control so that territorial

---

[17] John H. Herz, *op. cit.*, p. 89.
[18] Andrew M. Scott, *The Revolution in Statecraft: Informal Penetration*, Random Press, New York, 1965, p. 4.

boundaries may become of diminishing significance. What many states today fear, it is argued, is not so much overt armed attack across their territorial frontiers, but rather subversion from within and foreign sponsored *coups d'états*. Indeed, the very loyalty of its citizens to the state may be challenged 'by a trans-national appeal that seeks to reach out across national boundaries'. At times indeed the notion of the sovereign state as a 'self-contained decisional unit' comes to be challenged, whether through the presence of foreign nationals within the decision-making apparatus or through the capacity of an external power to direct the state's own nationals. All these forms of informal penetration, Andrew Scott argues, point to the 'progressive breakdown of the inviolable nation state'. It is an interesting thesis, skilfully deployed. Yet he does not envisage the disappearance of the nation-states, but rather a significant modification of their nature and functioning. Nor does it necessarily follow that the growing interpenetration of states will lead to an erosion either of their constitutional right to manage their own affairs or indeed of their actual capacity to do so. On the contrary, over the last few years the determination of even the smaller states to assert and maintain their control of their economies and their societies generally has been very marked, for many of the reasons that John Hertz has recognized. Despite the tragedy of Czechoslovakia in 1968 several other East European members of the socialist state system have steadily, albeit cautiously, managed to assert an increasing autonomy of political and economic decision-making. At the height of the cold war covert operations by the CIA and other forms of informal penetration were potent instruments in the United States armoury. With the advent of a measure of *détente* between the super-powers they have become considerably blunted. Moreover, their potency is in a large measure a function of the vulnerability of the target states. This vulnerability is often in turn a product of the lack of stability and cohesion in a state. As the regimes in the recently independent states consolidate their hold upon their populations, their vulnerability to external penetration can be expected to diminish. In any case, as Andrew Scott himself recognizes, informal penetration is far from being exclusively a 20th-century phenomenon. In fact, it could be argued that it has been characteristic of the international system of sovereign states almost from its inception in the 17th century.

There is the related argument focusing on the theme of neo-colonialism. Very briefly the argument is that political independence is meaningless without the achievement of economic independence.

There may be notional sovereignty in the sense of a state being generally recognized as sovereign in both legal and diplomatic theory, but factually it is dependent on an external power for the basic necessities of its existence whether in terms of economic need or political security. Nkrumah voiced his suspicion of the neo-colonialist designs of the former colonial powers when he argued that though they were 'prepared to grant political independence, their determination to maintain economic dominance deprived this independence of any real meaning'. Now it cannot be denied that for much of the first part of this century economic – and security – considerations mingled to produce a status of near political servitude in notionally independent states, whether they were the oil-producing states of the Middle East or 'banana republics' in Central America and the Caribbean. And there have been any number of instances of economic penetration being used as an instrument for establishing or consolidating a relationship of political subservience. There are also the critics of the association of Francophone African states with the European Economic Community under the Yaoundé Convention who regard such association as an instance of neo-colonialism – of notional independence, but factual subservience.

Yet on the whole the trend over the last decade has, in my view, been in the opposite direction. The socialization of many of the economies of the developing countries has in most instances made them less vulnerable to neo-colonialist pressures,[19] while the diplomatic and domestic support they can muster in resisting these pressures, together with the sellers' market which has developed in many of the resources which they command, has greatly enhanced their bargaining power whether with individual foreign governments or with foreign economic companies.[20] Even in the case of the associated states under the Yaoundé Convention the trend seems to be one of decreasing dependence on the former metropole and an increasing assertion of their identity as states whose sovereignty is not a mere façade.

Finally, there is the irruption on to the international stage of a major new set of actors, namely the multinational corporations, which 'sprawl across national boundaries, linking the assets and

[19] The right of host countries to nationalize or expropriate foreign owned companies is now generally conceded, and the latters' main preoccupation is with the terms of compensation.

[20] Witness the success of members of OPEC, especially when they present a united front.

activities of different national jurisdictions with an intimacy that seems to threaten the concept of the nation as an integral unit'.[21] This is a very large subject with an abundant literature. Nor is it, as Arnold Wolfers, Raymond Aron and others have remarked, a particularly new phenomenon except in terms of the increasing number of MNC's involved and the growing magnitude of their operations. Raymond Vernon has claimed that overseas subsidiaries of international enterprises 'may account for approximately 15 per cent of world production' and they are said to command reserve assets of the order of £100 billion. These 'invisible Empires'[22] or 'footloose giants', as Susan Strange points out, have 'developed a very sophisticated and specious ideology in which they are the international St Georges about to slay the dragon of nationalism'.[23] By many in Europe the multinational enterprise is on the contrary feared as an ally and harbinger of American hegemony, to be resisted for political and cultural reasons whatever the economic benefits it brings, while in developing countries the determination to assert national sovereignty over natural resources often takes precedence over the economic attractions such enterprises have to offer. The point is that most governments are often in something of a quandary. They 'badly want . . . not only a sense of control over foreign owned subsidiaries but also access to the resources they think some of these subsidiaries can provide'.[24] And these resources are to be seen not only in terms of investment capital, but also in terms of technological and managerial know-how and of access to markets. Yet behind the subsidiary lurks the spectre of the parent's power and the fear is that the growing scale of multinational corporations' operations may induce a degree of dependence on the part of host states which may circumscribe the exercise of their sovereignty in the economic realm. Control of some of the technological heights of the economy – electronics, automotive, chemical and pharmaceutical, and other industries – by foreign owned enterprises may hamper the management of the economy by the state and effectively inhibit the nationalization of companies whose operations are closely integrated with subsidiaries abroad. In particular, as the successive monetary crises of the last two years have shown only too vividly, the transfer

[21] Raymond Vernon, *Sovereignty at Bay*, Longmans, London, 1971, p. 5.

[22] Louis Turner, *Invisible Empires*, Hamilton, London, 1970.

[23] Susan Strange, 'International Economics and International Relations: A Case of Mutual Neglect', *International Affairs*, April 1970.

[24] Raymond Vernon, *op. cit.*, p. 247.

of short-term capital by multinational corporations in order to exploit changes in exchange rates has been a substantial element in the speculative movements of 'hot money' which have had a severely damaging impact on the whole international monetary system. A failure on the part of governments to exercise effective control of these movements could greatly limit their capacity to manage their own economies. *If* the latter were to come about – and on the whole, as Dennis Kavanagh suggests, the risks of this happening have been much exaggerated – this could constitute such a curtailment of the capacity of a number of sovereign states to exercise their sovereignty within the domestic economic realm as to call into question the very concept of their being sovereign, that is, of their capacity to exercise supreme authority within their territory.

To conclude, by summarizing very briefly. The first contention in this article is that although the concept of sovereignty can be given several different meanings, the most helpful is to treat it as an 'absolute and not a relative concept. There may be marginal cases and obscure situations, making it hard to say whether or not a state is constitutionally self-contained; but *in principle* it can only be one thing or the other. If it is not separate and supreme in constitutional terms, it lacks sovereignty. If it does enjoy these attributes, this is conclusive as to its sovereign status, no matter what its size or strength.'[25] Consequently, whatever constraints or pressures a state is subject to, however much its freedom of action be curtailed, a state remains sovereign so long as it retains these attributes of sovereignty. In diplomatic and legal convention there is a clear dividing line between being sovereign and not being sovereign. In principle, therefore, sovereignty cannot be eroded; it can only be extinguished.

The second contention – and concession – is that in political practice, i.e. in terms of the *capacity* of states to exercise the rights that stem from their sovereignty, the position may be less clear cut. A judgement whether the exercise of these rights by a particular state has been so curtailed as effectively to incapacitate its sovereignty calls for an analysis into the decision-making process within that state to ascertain whether the concepts of constitutional self-containment and separateness are still applicable. The term 'client' state or 'satellite' indicates that there may be cases in the past where they have not been; and there are those who argue that within the shade of a hegemonic power or under the yoke of economic tutelage the degree of dependence may be such as to deprive a notionally sovereign state

[25] Alan James, *op. cit.*, p. 18. Italics added.

of its effective decision-making capacity. But the argument here is that although there may indeed still be instances of what in practice might be held to constitute an erosion of sovereignty – i.e. instances of notional sovereignty but factual subservience – the number of such instances is probably declining, not increasing.

The third contention, therefore, is that in the world at large the sovereign state is still the basic political unit of international society, and this in terms not merely of diplomatic and legal convention but also of political realities. Other 'actors' have crept on to the international stage, particularly the multinational business companies, but they have not yet usurped the centre of that stage. The 'core' political actors and decision-makers in the world at large are still sovereign states. Even the thickening web of collaboration between states necessitated by security and welfare needs is still collaboration *between* sovereign entities; their freedom of choice may often be closely circumscribed, but as choose they must, so they choose as discrete and separate units. International organizations are still more arenas of diplomacy than instruments of government and the collaboration they have encouraged has strengthened rather than eroded the sovereignty of their members – by making it less of an anachronism than it might otherwise be. Consequently, peace is to be sought not by adumbrating blueprints premised upon the imminent demise of the sovereign state, but through some pragmatic mix of the recipes for reconciling the facts of state sovereignty with the requirements of international order traditionally offered by the rationalist and realist schools mentioned earlier.

The final contention – and again concession – is that on a *regional* level it is easier to conceive of ambiguous situations where it may not be altogether misleading to speak of the voluntary relinquishment of some of the attributes of sovereignty. Here the European Economic Community is particularly relevant. The interpenetration of the economies of the members of the Community, through the institution of a common market and the first tentative steps towards an economic union, has by no means submerged the constitutional identity of the member-states. And the assertion by the inter-governmental Council of Ministers of its central role in the Community decision-making process suggests that this identity is likely to persist – at least for some time to come. It is possible, however, that in Western Europe a process has been devised within which the domestic and external domains of sovereignty may become steadily so indistinguishable as to constitute the steady erosion of the decision-making capacity of the member-states to a point where their individual identity may be extinguished in favour of a new and larger sovereign entity. But this is another subject and, in any case, whether the Community process will evolve in this direction and whether, if it did so, it would necessarily conduce to world peace, still remains to be seen.

Luxemburgensis

The Emergence of a European Sovereignty

THE FACT THAT A PARALLEL CAN BE DRAWN BETWEEN THE PROCESS of European integration and an emerging sovereignty illustrates the political nature of European integration. No matter what definitions of sovereignty are used – and we will come back to that – it is clear that the European Community has one fundamental characteristic: it is a framework within which an attempt is being made to translate into action, through an institutional process, a complex of economic, social, and human aspirations. If politics consist in making possible what is desirable, then the Community does indeed deal with politics. What is important is the degree of originality and autonomy in the community, rather than references to such notions as 'subject to international law' or 'political recognition'. Much has been written on the concept of sovereignty and on various aspects of its changing nature. One need not go as far as Politis:[1] 'Sovereignty has already been virtually abolished and if the word is still used in official and, to a lesser extent, scientific language, this is due to the failure to adapt visually, to the disappearance of a light which for long has burnt so brightly.' If it can be said that the notion of *bon plaisir*, applied by an extreme anthropomorphic transfer to a state, is disappearing in the western world, it remains none the less true that important traits of sovereignty continue to be ideas which must be reckoned with and they exist in fact, or in men's minds (which sometimes comes to the same thing).

Thus it can be said that the following characteristics of sovereignty remain (even in changing forms):

– on the internal plane, the organization must be statist; it must

[1] Politis: *Le problème des limitations de souveraineté* in *Recueil de Cours*, Vol. 6, 1925, pp. 5 ff. and p. 10.

comprise a complex of subjects and aspirations and a decision-making process which enables the basic aspirations to materialize, if need be even against minority positions.
– on the external plane, the organization must be able to deploy itself. Although it is not indispensable that it should be recognized as a state, at least it should be accepted by other states outside as a reality and even perhaps as a partner in international affairs.

The fact that a body such as the European Community can be subjected to internal influences and pressures (for example, by governments or by multinational corporations) or to external ones (the influence of other states through certain member-states) does not mean that the notion of sovereignty should be discounted. The same thing happens also within the nation-states, without their existence being called in question. It has never occurred to anyone to deny recognition to a state merely because it depends upon one or two basic materials which are in the hands of a foreign company or because its defence, let alone its foreign relations, are taken over by law or in fact by another state.

With regard to the Community, on the other hand, certain limitations – although they may often be less clear – are put forward to cast doubt upon the existence of the genuine autonomy of the system. This is, on the whole, understandable in that the Community by reason of its constitution, its objectives, and its methods, does not directly dwell upon the issue of internal and external sovereignty. To the extent to which the Community's powers are limited, its methods gradual, founded on the articulation of relations between states, the terms of comparison cannot be those of the traditional concept of 'sovereignty'. Very often the first act of a country (for example, after secession) is to proclaim its internal and external sovereignty. In the Community's case, sovereignty is largely the outcome of the effective functioning of the system and of its achievements.

After a brief look at the Community from the point of view of its constitution, we will see how it works, bearing in mind its specific characteristics. Finally we shall try to draw up a balance-sheet between the loss of sovereignty of the member-states and the gain of sovereignty within the Community.

THE CONSTITUTIONAL NATURE OF THE COMMUNITY

Political scientists have rightly placed at the heart of the problem the question as to whether the Community is irreversible. Article 240 of the EEC states that the treaty has been concluded *sine die*. The treaty can only be modified by common consent and only after the institution itself (the Council) has decided.

The problem of the Common Market's irreversibility is usually seen in the light of a possible disintegration of the whole. Its history has not confirmed these gloomy predictions. To be sure, in the picture which is often drawn of sovereignty with regard to the Community, the notion of the whole complex is seen as a peculiar characteristic. From this, it follows that some unrealized ambitions, abandoned initiatives or postponements are seen, in varying degrees, as denials of the irreversible nature of the Community. But the failures and delays, no matter how bitter they may have been, have not been regarded by the Community as hindrances to the process of integration, but rather as encouragements to follow up integration by different methods. Should crises or tensions arise around existing Community policies, and should the Community be driven in on itself and fail to take the matter up again in the form of fresh actions and perspectives, then a decisive blow against its irreversibility would have been struck.

Most observers agree that the Community is irreversible, by reason of the links and networks which have been established. Some disagree. It is doubtful, therefore, if any useful purpose can be served by prolonging the discussion on this point, since in any case the argument will only cease when all the clashes and postponements within the Community have disappeared, or when – an unlikely event – it has achieved the status of a state seated by right in the General Assembly of the United Nations.

It must be remembered, too, that in many states tensions between opposing groups and rival regions are played out against the backcloth of a possible break up of the whole. In a world in which arguments of this kind become more and more bitter, who would want to deprive himself for ever of this supreme weapon of dissuasion and who, for that matter, could guarantee that such a thing would never happen?

The treaties have a constitutional aspect in that they express political aims and envisage a *dialectic of powers* by which their policy is put into practice. The Community is the *legal person* on the internal and external plane (Article 210). The laws of the Community are imposed directly (or indirectly) upon the member-states and private parties. These constitutional characteristics are undeniable, but they tend to be disputed in terms of sovereignty, when it comes to putting them into practice. The legal order peculiar to the Community has been validated by the courts of justice, especially the court of the European Community.

The Community has been granted sectors of activity in which it alone can act. This implies the *withdrawal of the member-states* from a number of external capacities (common policy in trade; agreements of association; negotiations on definite internal policies). It is for the Community, too, to pronounce on certain taxes, on agreements between enterprises, on the tariffs in support of enterprises, etc. In so far as common policies are defined, the Community becomes responsible for implementing them and disposes of the power to modify them. Vast sectors of human activity have thus gradually come within the competence of the Community.

Side by side with these areas of exclusive responsibility, there are a growing number of areas of joint responsibilities, shared between the Community and the member-states. This is particularly noticeable in the realm of regional, social, and industrial policy.

The evolutionary character of the Community's responsibilities is confirmed by the facts and noted in the treaties. The Community has gradually extended its horizons, using at first more cautious methods and ending up, in some cases, with decision-making procedures in the fullest sense of the term. The treaty provides for this in Article 235, which gives the institutions the necessary powers to implement the policies which derive from its objects. Social legislation and environmental matters are examples of this.

Of course, the limitation of sovereignty acquiesced in by the member-states, especially in international agreements, does not imply that the new entity itself has acquired its own powers. For example, the member-states may agree not to empty waste matter into the sea. The body dealing with this may even have the power to lay down rules concerning what waste can be emptied into the sea. The member-states may therefore have ceded to such organizations a large portion of their authority in specific matters. But this agreed loss of sovereignty does not lead to the emergence of a new sovereignty. The powers given to the organs of Eurocontrol are wide, but we cannot speak here of a new sovereignty. For the notion of sovereignty to be taken into account the authority must cover a large part of human activity. It is the extent of this field of action which enables links and arbitrations between different interests to operate.

Without a minimal sense of the common good and of a common allegiance no autonomous action is conceivable. If sovereignty is abandoned and powers allocated elsewhere for technical reasons, a new sovereignty does not necessarily emerge. But if the reaction to events leads to a common action and thus those whose task it is to defend the common good can play their part, then autonomy and sovereignty begin to emerge.

Redistribution, in different forms, which is the expression of the solidarity of the members, is a basic characteristic of sovereignty conceived in this sense.

Lastly, *the behaviour of the actors* must be conditioned by the needs of the whole rather than by the different points of departure of those who take a purely national point of view.

In so far as the actors are under pressure from public opinion and in so far as public opinion can be informed and influenced by the body whose task it is to promote the Community – in this case, the Commission – a popular current is introduced into the process – in contrast to diplomatic attitudes. This is a necessary condition of an emerging sovereignty which cannot ignore the pressure of the man in the street. The pressure of public opinion therefore weighs heavily upon the Commission and the Council. Side by side with trends of opinion (rare) in support of a national position, transnational currents in support of various solutions appear.

To be sure, public pressure finds its most 'sovereign' expression in a parliament elected directly by universal suffrage (something which the Community possesses only in principle).

Popular pressure in the Community (one of the characteristics of internal sovereignty) is sufficiently pronounced for it to be possible to speak of the beginning of sovereignty; indeed it can make itself felt more powerfully than in many countries whose 'sovereignty' is beyond dispute.

It can, therefore, be said that the system itself contains the seeds of autonomy and sovereignty. But does not the way in which this power emerges cast doubt upon its autonomy?

THE EVOLUTION OF SOVEREIGNTY

The most debatable point about the uniqueness of the Community is that it is based on the member-states and especially the national governments. This is true as far as the process of decision-making is concerned, but is realized to a great extent in the participation in the carrying out of decisions which have been taken.

This point must therefore be examined more closely in the light of the whole context of the environment within which the Community operates. The fact is that the members of two of the three Institutions are appointed by the governments unanimously. Although there are no representatives of the member-states in the Commission and in the Court of Justice, yet the treaties provide that a minimum number of nationals from each country should be appointed to both these Institutions.

The members of the Commission cannot be removed for the duration of their mandate, unless by disciplinary action or by a vote of no confidence in the European Parliament. They neither ask for, nor receive, any kind of directives and are supposed to act completely independently in the general interest of the Community. (The members of the European Parliament are made up of delegates chosen by the national parliaments from their own midst, although the governments are not without influence on the method of selection.)

It might be tempting to stress the conditions of appointment of the members of Institutions, called upon to represent the common interest rather than the way in which these members carry out their duties – a way which should be 'European'. Is it naive to speak of the genuine independence and authority shown by those who are invested with these offices? This is neither the time nor the place to make a study of the behaviour of the members of the executive and the holders of judicial office. This author, speaking for himself, starts from the assumption that, beginning with a certain level of functions and a certain political or administrative level, men prefer to exercise fully the functions entrusted to them rather than to watch the erosion of the moral credit upon which their careers are based.

There is nothing exceptional in the fact that the members of the executives and of the judiciary are appointed by the governments since in those states in which the members of the highest offices or of certain constitutional bodies are appointed by the governments, the method of appointment is rarely given as grounds for questioning the autonomy of those who are appointed, or, to go one step further, the autonomy of the system. Their nomination by the government is more than counter-balanced by the fact that they must work with the members of the Council and of the governments of all the member-states and that their success depends largely upon the support of the public which does not approve of partisan views.

Is not the Commission, assuming that the members are independent, forced when making decisions to do what the member-states demand? Does not the well-known realism of the Commission

lie finally in proposing what is acceptable to the lowest common de-
nominator or what can be achieved by using more or less instant
coalitions between the most varied interests? Can it not even be said
that the close contacts made by the Commission in the drawing up of
their proposals place these within the lines drawn by the experts of
the different member-states?

Such a danger is undeniably virtually inherent in the system. The
Commission, just as the government of a western-type industrialized state, is confronted by an enormous number of problems
which it must resolve by fitting its decisions into a unified complex of
policies, without being itself able to take every decision. It follows
that the Commission, if it wants to remain at the centre of things,
must put forward proposals which can further integration, naturally,
but which are also such as will be supported by the member-states.
Inevitably therefore the experts of the member-states play a great
part during the phase when the position of the Commission is being
drawn up. Nevertheless, in many cases there is disagreement between
the services and the appropriate cabinets of the Commission and the
experts of the member-states (which are not involved at this stage)
which the Commission must settle. What is more important is the
realization that in those matters which involve the Community's
future, the Commission alone is responsible. It is with regard to these
proposals that the political nature is asserted of the Commission's
right to initiate and it is also in regard to these proposals that the
Commission is directly engaged with the Ministers in the Council,
often without the shield of an intermediary body.[2]

The fact that the member-states are directly associated, through
the procedure known as administrative committees, with current administration and implementation of the Council's rulings, is not in
itself likely to restrict the largely autonomous way in which the
Commission applies the community law. The Commission's position
in these committees is very strong for constitutional, as well as for
technical reasons (knowledge of files; comradeship at work) so that
the number of decisions arrived at which are contested by the member-states and have to be brought before the Council remain at about
one in a thousand.

The national governments naturally find their most open field of
expression within the Council. Here again the question arises as to
whether the Council can work as an autonomous body, rising above

[2] In 1972 the Commission met with governmental and private experts during
its sessions.

the sum of the initial positions of the delegations of which it is composed.

On the negative side, it cannot be said that the beginning of a new sovereignty can be seen in the Community. On the affirmative side, it can be said that the tensions within it are the natural expression of a federal or a pre-federal system which is constitutionally characterized by the struggle between the federation, eager to increase its powers, and the states which form it which are anxious to retain as much as possible of their autonomy.

The very fact that the member-states are in different degrees eager to maintain their prerogatives is not an argument against the genuineness of the system. However, if this eagerness were to lead to the blocking of decisions or their deflection in the direction of negotiations of the classical kind, it would not be possible to speak of an emerging sovereignty. The Communitarian process has been examined in an impressive number of studies and the course taken by some proposals has been the object of almost clinical analyses. Attempts at quantification and qualification of the whole are, on the other hand, rarer. This is because the minutes of the Council, like those of the Commission, are not published and such a study can only be carried out on the basis of a complete documentation, extending over a fairly long period of time.

This being said, the first criterion of the characteristic autonomy of the system is that of its effectiveness.

From the quantitative point of view, the reserve of decisions not accepted by the Council corresponds by and large to the sum of proposals submitted in one year. If one cannot therefore speak of the ineffectiveness of the proposals in quantitative terms, neither can one question the efficacy of the proposals in terms of the results actually obtained in the Council. The Commission's right to amend its proposal and the Council's right to amend the Commission's proposal are fundamental to the system. Both the Council and the Commission use this right freely. But this being said, there are very few instances of the Council simply rejecting one of the Commission's proposals. Thus, one can count on one's fingers the proposals which the Council has modified to such an extent that they have differed substantially from the one put forward by the Commission. Normally, the Commission adapts its proposal to make it acceptable to the Council, without going so far as to abandon any of the principles upon which it is based.

While preferring to leave to others the task of making quantitative and qualitative analyses of the function of the proposal, it can safely be said that every initiative in the Community has been taken in the Commission and that every proposal has borne the profound imprint of its action. Some proposals have been accepted as they stood, others have been modified over the years, under different initiatives.

The Commission exerts its influence through media suitable for political action (contacts with professionals, seminars, conferences, and press communiques; interventions in the European Parliament and in the Economic and Social Committee, 'green papers'), the whole operation being designed to detect popular aspirations and to assure popular support for its policies. The margin of support which the Commission enjoys is proportional to the degree of popular allegiance in Europe to the Community and to the spirit of solidarity the people are ready to show. Innumerable public opinion polls in Europe indicate that there is basic support for the process of integration upon which the Commission can count. Of course, it is not to be expected that public opinion will mobilize itself in favour of Europe, beyond the point at which it is engaged nationally. Yet it is always on the issues which reveal the fragility of the Community that public opinion reacts most strongly – for the Community is never immune from challenge or crisis (unlike most countries which will remain whatever happens).

This, then, is the political role of proposals by the Commission, which can help to crystallize positions and produce the 'drama'. Hence arise too the attempts to restrict the right to propose. It is because the right of proposal can have such an influence on the formulation of the decision that it is only fully recognized to the Commission in questions which are the object of a fundamental consensus – be it matters which are formally written into the treaty or matters which it has been agreed to incorporate gradually within this framework.

These elements, though important, render less acute the problem of the majority vote in the Council, although this remains one of the touch-stones of the system. Indeed, the opportunities for action in the Communitarian system, and the rules of the game, are fundamentally different according to whether the debate takes place in terms of a majority vote or in terms of the maintenance of the rule of unanimity. It must be noted in this respect that the Community is a body in which the vote is very frequently used. This is true of the Commission itself and of the many committees which surround it for the implementation of the Council's regulations. Even though the

Council has appeared somewhat grudging in allocating competence for the making of secondary community law, it must nevertheless be recognized that, on the whole, the Commission has been given executive powers which are largely comparable to those which a national government receives from its parliament.

If we add to these current questions those on which there is a regular vote in the Council (questions of procedure and finance; staff and statutory affairs) and taking into consideration decisions for which unanimity is legally necessary (see Article 100 and Article 235/EEC) it can be seen that the limit within which an effective vote can be cast is relatively narrow (by restricting 'vital' matttes, i.e. subjects upon which neither the Commission nor the member-states would ever dream of being outvoted for the sake of it). The fact is that for these intermediate questions, the Council has resorted more frequently to the vote. Moreover, now that it has been enlarged to nine, it seems to be showing a sort of defensive reflex, and accepts the recourse to the vote more readily and especially resorts to a show of hands, from which the partners may draw their own conclusions.

The problem then of the qualified majority cannot be given a definite answer in one sense or the other.

Can the member-states themselves decide whether a problem is a Community matter or remains within the jurisdiction of the member-states? The Community has not been spared conflicts over authority as between states and 'federation'. It must be admitted that every time there has been opposition of a political and theoretical kind between the Commission, on the one hand, and one or more member-states on the other over these matters, it has been more often than not the governmental rather than the federal authority which has dominated. The concern of the member-states, shared more or less tacitly by the Commission, has always been not to endanger possible practical progress for the sake of maintaining institutional positions leading to inflexibility. This attitude has been facilitated by the Commission's profound conviction that the pressure of events will, in the end, change the outlook of recalcitrant states, and that in such matters it is better to govern with events than against them. The Community's evolution has done nothing to prove the Commission mistaken about this.

In conclusion, the participation of the member-states in the decision-making, as well as the conflicts over authority, are quite simply inherent in any federal-type system. The genuine and 'sovereign' character of the Community does not spring from the system so much as from the way it has been applied. In this respect, it is difficult to deny the emergence of a sovereignty, though one cannot assert that the Communitarian system works with all the completeness which characterizes a strong government.

One cannot help being struck by the fact that appreciation of the unique character of the Community varies according to whether it is seen from the angle of member-states, of states outside the Community or of the industrial enterprises. While the governments and administrations of the member-states have very precise views on the powers delegated to the Commission, they remain firmly convinced that, on the whole, they themselves hold the reins of the system subject to a continuous battle in defence of their own interests and prerogatives. This attitude is based very largely upon the conviction that what the Commission proposes – and which has a fair chance of success – falls within the range of what is tolerable.

Although the dialectical tensions thus set up, are not of a revolutionary nature, nevertheless they show that the system has reached a definite degree of maturity. They convince the member-states that they are participating fully in the game and are 'at home' in the Community. Those who see the system from further away, for example business circles and nations outside it, tend to discern more easily its uniqueness and character.

On the plane of economic reactions, many sectors have outstripped the institutional aspect of the EEC. There have been many instances of multinational companies, especially those whose decision-making centres are outside the Community, anticipating what the Community was to become and orientating their policy in terms of this new factor.

On the more formal plane of recognition, the non-member states have, from the first, sent diplomatic missions to the High Authority. For the countries of the West, the conclusion of agreements with the Community has been regarded as a natural outcome of 'recognition', regardless of any positive support which any of them may have intended to give to the Community, as a partner in international affairs. Thus with reference to non-member states, the 'reality' of the Community no longer seems to be in doubt. There remains among some of them, however, the problem of accepting the Community as a partner in international affairs.

But the absence of recognition and the refusal to consider the Community as a partner is more and more seldom put forward as an argument for the lack of reality and of uniqueness in the Community.

Thus, when 'recognition' is refused systematically and for political reasons the refusal in itself serves to give more prominence to the whole problem; in the long run the refusal to make political realities coincide with political recognition leads to frustrated, and even schizophrenic attitudes.

It can even be said that the member-states are more reluctant to give up 'sovereignty' in external matters than in internal matters. The history of relations between the Commission, the Council and the member-states which led to the decision of the Court of Justice on the ERTA,[3] as well as the events which followed illustrate this point.

Undeniably, the processes of integration which, in themselves tend to reduce the importance of the diplomatic function in the classic sense in relations between the member-states have given rise to a new way of co-ordinating the positions of the member-states which is conducted, in general, by those who have been in charge of classic diplomatic relations. It would be unrealistic to expect of them a spontaneous adherence to full recognition of the Community with all the consequences which this would entail for the role of the Commission. Thus the gradual filling in of the external contours of the Community has followed the laws of functional development, and internal resistance against external pressures has possibly been stronger than in many other fields. The Commission has taken this into account, by devising a whole panoply of procedures running from the exclusive representation of the Community by itself alone (for example, the final phase of the Geneva negotiations) to the proposal for mixed delegations, let alone negotiations conducted in the name of the member-states in a co-ordinated form. The member-states often hesitate to take the final step – this is especially true in new fields such as financial relations – and confer the role of spokesman on the then President of the Council, rather than on the Commission as the constituted negotiator, which would be equivalent to recognition of a handing over of authority. The Commission has put no obstacle in the way of these formulae, realizing that they they are transitory and that in time the need for external coherence will end by imposing a single negotiator.

The recognition of the existence of the Community in all its internal and external implications also implies a choice in favour of the federal power with which a body such as the Community is obliged to live, but which cannot come about suddenly through a political

[3] European Road Transport Agreement.

decision. On the other hand, the Community's attributions are a function of what its partners are willing to confer on it, and thus they appear in the eyes of the latter as delegated tasks rather than as tasks originating in the Community.

It must be added that in a pre-federal system which is taking shape, change cannot take place without some prerogatives and privileges which have hitherto been firmly held, passing into other hands; moreover, these transfers must take place in a Western-type society in which the maintenance of acquired rights is erected into a dogma. It follows that such transfers can be spread over a generation of officials, and indeed may only take place after the departure of an official who was too attached to his own fief. The tendencies towards resistance are compensated for by the fact that the non-member states have an even stronger tendency to see the Community as an entity and to endow it with responsibilities which in turn leads it to behave as an entity.

We come now to the question whether it is possible to draw a parallel between the notion of government in a national setting and in the setting of the Community. The nature of the 'decision' which the Community can make in comparison to that of a government does not appear at first sight to be a fundamental distinction. In Western-type democracies, the governments' room for manoeuvre is in fact very restricted and the results which they reach depend to a great extent on choices of the moment, on the political regrouping of interests, on the account taken of public opinion and of the influences upon it, on the support of organized interests, etc.

If it is true that because of the objections of a member-state, some actions have not been undertaken at Community level, it is also true that others could not have been undertaken except through the Community. Similarly, one cannot really state *a priori* that the quality of decisions in the Commission is superior or inferior to what takes place within the member-states; in fact, many things cannot be solved within the national framework so the question is superfluous.

The Communitarian system has granted the Commission a greater power of innovation which is wider than that of the national governments, bound by their daily activities and limited by public opinion. One can of course reproach the Community for passing its decisions in package-deals in which the most varied elements are mixed. At the same time, there is a tendency to lose sight of the fact that, within the national framework, decisions are also made in package deals, for instance in the governmental programmes which are negotiated at the beginning of each session.

The difference between the Community and the national states in this respect may lie rather in the extent of the stratification of problems linked to each other than in the nature of the Community. Moreover the need to consider public opinion is common to both systems. The proof of this is the part taken by the Community in the press and the crowd of journalists who besiege the Council when it meets.

THE RELATIÓNSHIP BETWEEN THE LOSS OF SOVE-REIGNTY OF THE MEMBER-STATES AND THE GAIN OF SOVEREIGNTY OF THE COMMUNITY

If sovereignty was considered as a mass one could examine its distribution between the member-states and the Community, and analyse the changes in this distribution taking place over time. *A priori*, one might be tempted to suggest that the traditional manifestations of internal and external sovereignty (i.e. the possibility of taking judicial decisions which are directly applicable; the accreditation of ambassadors) are indivisible acts, which would mean that as the role of the Community increased that of the member-states would be reduced and *vice versa*. This is no doubt true from the point of view of the traditional manifestation of sovereignty, but far less so if the decision-making in the Community is taken into account as well as the fluctuating nature of the powers of the Community.

The problem is seen in a quite different light when a different definition of sovereignty is taken as the starting-point: the capacity of a body to transform the aspirations of a whole entity into political actions which can lead to decisions. In such a case one might well speak of sovereignty at Community level (for example, to be the spokesman in negotiations with the United States on the organization of world trade; to settle the level at which enriched uranium should be stored for peaceful purposes) without such sovereignty being exercised at the level of the individual states. Inversely, the state regains a part of its national power by working from within the complex. Insofar as a state which can only act within the complex finds it closed to its aspirations, a kind of frustration sets in comparable in nature to the reactions of individuals and collectivities faced with an impotent state. The problem of 'missed sovereignty' within the Community might thus be more real than that of sovereignties 'dominated' by the grip of the Community system (for instance by the recourse to the vote by a qualified majority).

One may speak of 'lost sovereignty' when the degree of integration achieved makes it impossible for the member-states to settle some problems among themselves which they were free to settle formerly and when the Community itself takes no action to settle them. This situation can arise when international competition prevents one state from taking alone the internal measures which seem desirable to it, but it can also arise when the decisions which have already been taken by the Community are not flexible enough to take account of the changing factors.

Again, it is because operational 'sovereignty' can also only work through the whole entity that a state may be tempted to deflect from within the behaviour of the entity in order to make it serve special interests, for instance, particular engagements which it may have taken with regard to nations outside.

The scene is further complicated by the collision between motivations founded on the need to respect the external manifestations of sovereignty and the necessities springing from the need for action. In such a case a member-state can block every proposal for action by the whole entity on the grounds that it would lose its sovereign attributions (in the traditional but not effective sense). The intensity with which 'missed sovereignty' is felt by the other partners depends not only on the extent of the missed opportunities but is proportional to the degree of arbitrariness inherent in an attachment to external values which are no longer based upon reality.

Thus the Community has speeded up the need to exercise sovereignty in action on the level of the entity as a whole, but at the same time the starting points – often inspired by the anxiety to preserve external signs of past positions – have introduced brakes into the system.

The refusal to make the external manifestations of sovereignty coincide with the demands of functional sovereignty creates a field of tensions into which the Commission can insert itself in order to bend the member-states towards making a more supple mechanism of decision, and towards institutional progress.

It is difficult to deny that the way in which functional sovereignty works and expresses itself depends largely on the type of social organization to which it is applied and on the procedures according to which the body draws up its decisions.

It is therefore premature to attempt to answer the question as to what will be the external manifestations of the sovereignty of a Community which is gradually coming to exercise the functions expected of it. The institutional form devised for the whole complex will depend on the type of society towards which we are travelling. The real question is thus whether the Communitarian system will speed up this evolution and whether it follows a creative line. Decision-making by 'concertation' which is characteristic of our society, as opposed to the notion of 'command' naturally attached to the notion of a leader, offers to the Community the opportunities for action and innovation which can be, in many cases, more genuine than those of which national leaders can make use, who are naturally inclined to solve first the immediate problems facing their electorates.

From the point of view of the questions discussed here, the important thing is that the peoples and the political leaders should be convinced that the problem is looked at and can be solved in a 'European' way. The delays and failures registered so far have most often been caused by the resistance of those elements which hold the technical levers in the member-states and in industry, and which have resisted any change which might jeopardize their own positions. In one way or another, these refusals are the expression of attachment to the manifestations of past sovereignty. Without minimizing the effect of these brakes, it must be recognized however that they cannot in the long run stand up against public pressure and the political will of the leaders, upon both of which the Commission and the Parliament have considerable influence. The Community's history is studded with fallen taboos. In the Community, crises have become a kind of natural pulsation. Whenever the need to act has been resisted there is a crisis, giving the Commission an opening for action. At the risk of pushing the paradox a little too far, one can say that the reluctance of the Community to invest itself with a form of classical sovereignty gives rise to its new process of sovereignty. In many respects, the process of overgenerating can be applied to the technique of integration. The vicissitudes of the Western currency during the last few years are a good example of the burgeoning sovereignty in the Community. What had heretofore been a matter practically excluded from the Community on the grounds of sovereignty has gradually become a policy disciplined in common, although that common discipline may have zig-zagged and changed course. The need to domesticate together currency on the one hand, and the resistance, global and political to monetary integration on the other, give to the Commission room to manoeuvre towards a closer union of the whole. The very fact that the possibility of creating monetary parity unilaterally within the Community is being discussed, in itself illustrates the change of mind which has come about. The most hopeful sign of an emerging sovereignty can be found in the popular reactions to governments whose policies could lead to a sort of self-excommunication. The demonstration of sovereignty made by a member-state, if it ultimately fails because it cannot resist the rationale of the common action, proves the strength of the momentum of the common action.

The history of the Community underlines that it has hardly been able – for reasons inherent in every federal system – to manifest 'sovereignty' with the sole aim of obtaining its recognition. The manifestations of internal and external sovereignty have been expressed only much later on the formal plane, the character of emergent sovereignty residing very much more in the feeling of allegiance to a policy carried out in common, a feeling which triumphed over the manifold trials of strength with which it was confronted.

The capacity to act, which appears in the long run to be the only valid criterion of sovereignty is won in this way every day. From this point of view the Community would seem to have brought to its members a net gain of sovereignty.

Translated from French

Two Views from Eastern Europe

After the main papers had been received and sent to the Secretariat of the International Political Science Association for circulation, the rapporteurs of the Commission were asked to consider two supplementary papers, each of which originated from a country in Eastern Europe. The authors of these papers proposed to present and circulate them at the IPSA Congress in Montreal. The papers were subsequently accepted as auxiliary material and the rapporteurs were invited to present them. The first paper was submitted by Professor Karel Pomaizl of the Czechoslovak Academy of Sciences, Institute for Philosophy and Sociology, Prague. Professor Pomaizl however did not attend the meeting and his paper was introduced by another member of the panel. The second paper under the title 'Sovereignty and the Co-operation of the States' was presented by Professor Ioan Ceterchi from the University of Bucharest, Romania. Professor Ceterchi was present at Montreal and took part in the discussion.

In the following pages we are presenting extracts from these two papers. (The extracts from Professor Ceterchi's paper were translated from the original version in French.)

EXTRACTS FROM PROFESSOR IOAN CETERCHI'S PAPER

'The nation-states are the result of national movements. They are based on the concept of nation or of nationality. In order to examine the problem of the nation, one has to start from the materialist-dialectic and historical theses of the evolution of society according to which the nation is the product of a complex historical process with a progressive character. The nation appears in history in a period of high development of human society and becomes itself a powerful factor for the progress and the civilization of the world.'

'The nation can be defined as the highest form of ethnical community in the contemporary and modern era, formed as an independent unit within the borders of a territory on the basis of its national economy, having an etatist political organization (represented by the nation-state) as well as a specific spiritual life expressed in the language, the psychology, the culture and the consciousness of the nation . . .'

'As can easily be seen from the analysis of the realities of the different countries of the world, the process of formation of the nation-states and of the nations is far from being completed. In some zones one may say that this process is only in its initial phase. But even in the developed countries where the nation has a long historical past, it can be noted that the national feeling, the defence of independence and of national sovereignty are primordial factors on the road to democratic transformation and social progress.'

'We consider that the process of formation of the nation-states, of the achievement of national unity continues to be an essential task for an important part of the world and that, in contemporary international circumstances, the fight against foreign domination and for the achievement of national unity forms an integral part of the general fight against imperialism, colonialism and neo-colonialism. The era of the socialist revolutions, of the passage of mankind from capitalism to socialism is also indissolubly linked with the necessity of the assertion of the nation at a higher level and linked also to a true national revival . . .'

'But at the same time in the contemporary world the need for cooperation between states is greater than ever before . . . Many national interests can be better achieved by the intermediary of cooperation with other nations. The increase in number of the international organizations and agencies has been impressive, especially since the second world war. But the increased number of international organizations does not however imply a decline of sovereignty. The nations joined international organizations for national reasons so as to further their individual interests . . .'

'It is a reality of our days that international relations in general and especially economic relations are not based exclusively on equitable relations, but that there are also unjust relations between dominant economies and subordinated economies. The attempts to transform this into a law of economic development, or indeed to transform it into a law of satellization of the weaker economies in relation to the dominant economy amounts to an attempt to divide up international economic co-operation in favour of certain closed economic groupings, dominated by some more powerful partners, and thus to deprive nations of their freedom of action . . .'

'The dimensions of the present technical and scientific revolution would make it impossible for some countries and especially for the small and medium sized countries still developing, to make use of the advances of these technological revolutions for their national interests if they were unable to draw on the collaboration and co-operation with other states. Yet this collaboration must not be equated with an internationalization of the forces of production which would require a self-limitation of the independence of the states, by the transfer of a part of their sovereignty to international organs, endowed with competences which belong properly to the sovereign power of the states. In economic co-operation and collaboration between states such problems as the making of economic policy, the determination of the principal proportions and rhythms of production, the distribution of the national income between accumulation and consumption, the foreign trade policy and the monetary policy, are problems which commit the present and the future of each country and which must be solved in conditions in which the state holds all the levers of the economic, political and social orientation of the country concerned . . .'

'The revolution of collaboration and co-operation between the states of the international community in very varied fields is based on the interest of the different states in participating more actively in the international division of labour, as well as on their belief that economic isolationism and autarkic policies go against their national interests. International collaboration is part of a conception which transforms co-operation into an instrument of common progress which gives an equal right to all the members to share in the advantages of contemporary civilization, and which prevents it from degenerating into an instrument of interference in the internal affairs of the partners, and of restraint on their economic and political independence.'

'The essential condition to observe so that collaboration between states should not lead to the emergence or intensification of relations of dependence is that relations between states, as a whole, regardless of their social system, should be based on the fundamental principles of contemporary international law, i.e., respect for national sovereignty and independence, full equality of rights, non-interference in the internal affairs of other countries, and the resort to peaceful means for solving differences instead of force or the threat of force.'

'Sovereignty, as the specific attribute of the state, finds its expression in the right of the state to solve freely and according to its own judgement its internal and external problems, without violating the rights of other states and the principles and the norms of international law . . .'

'In opposition to authors who hold that sovereignty is an obsolete concept, an obstacle in the way of peace and international collaboration, Romanian political scientists, together with other scholars from socialist or other socio-political regimes, remain constant upholders of the principle of national sovereignty, because it is only respect for the sovereignty of all states and collaboration and co-operation between nations, free, independent and equal in rights, which can guarantee peace and international security.'

'In conclusion, the sovereign states remain the principal actors in international relations. The sovereign state continues to be the best instrument for ensuring the civilization and the progress of the nations.'

'The states feel the objective need for co-operation. Each state wishes to decide for itself how much and what kind of co-operation with other nations is desirable within the framework of mutual interdependence.'

'Though sovereignty may continue to be a controversial concept, it is undoubtedly the foundation of the nation-state and of the world system.'

EXTRACTS FROM PROFESSOR KAREL POMAIZL'S PAPER*

'If refusing – as Marxists – the opinion on national and state sovereignty as a cause of conflicts and wars, and not regarding the way to world peace simply as its abolition or its exchange by integration, it does not at all mean that we should close our eyes to real problems of the relation between the national, the international and the supranational. We regard it, however, in another way.'

'As a consequence of uneven development in the world, there exist at present time nations and countries, which find themselves on different historical developmental levels. In those nations that are still consolidating themselves . . . national and state sovereignty has a full historical justification and enormous political importance. It provides them with the possibility of independent and free development, of catching up on their retardation behind others, entering contracts with others on the basis of equal rights and participating

* The extracts reproduced here from Professor Pomaizl's paper are taken from the English text as printed in Prague, and circulated at the IPSA conference which Professor Pomaizl did not attend.

actively in international policy. It is, therefore, a marked feature of their freedom and simultaneously an important instrument of strengthening and securing it. The demand to abolish their national and state sovereignty represents for them unavoidably an effort to prevent their free and independent development. It represents an illusory endeavour to skip a necessary stage in their development. It is an attempt to bring them to higher, international, supranational and, finally, humanitarian forms not in a natural way, on the basis of their own experience and voluntariness, but artificially, under the control of others and even by using force.'

'The defence of national and state sovereignty against similar attempts is not at all a form of national egoism by the name of which it often goes. On the contrary, it is necessary to qualify as a real national egoism the attempts to deprive them of their national and state sovereignty, undertaken by those who were their rulers yesterday (or belonged to the world that ruled them), who do not want to become reconciled to the loss of their supremacy, who try to hinder their free development in all possible ways, look down upon them patronizingly and defame them. The endeavour to present the adherence of these nations and countries to their own sovereignty as dangerous for world peace is just as ill-contrived as hypocritical: as though not unfreedom, but freedom were dangerous for peace.'

'Besides nations which are only originating and consolidating themselves, there are, however, in the contemporary world nations which have already reached their basic national aspirations, which have their economy, policy, culture, their state, etc., and are inasmuch developed that the national framework becomes tight for them. They surpass it in all spheres of social life and tend to what is called, according to circumstances, more or less precisely, internationality or supranationality.'

'However, integration is a fact which demands, even from the Marxists, not only a generally theoretical but also a practical viewpoint. The special conditions of the situation after World War II in which progressive anti-fascist forces had to put national sovereignty in the first place; the development of socialism in individual countries which inherited considerable backwardness from capitalism and were, moreover, disturbed and badly damaged by war; the necessity of defending not only socialist countries, but also the working people in capitalist countries against the world-ruling efforts of the USA; at first, the Marxists as well as Communist Parties were led by all these facts to refuse integration in general, to stress just the maintenance of national and state sovereignty against it. This viewpoint, which after all contradicts Lenin's opinions, could not be maintained. Integration is an unavoidable trend which is progressive in itself, it is made reactionary by capitalism which gives its impress to it. If opposing integration in general, we should find ourselves in the same position as those who destroyed machines in the 19th century and tried to prevent large-scale production of machines in factories, as they erroneously saw in it and not in the capitalist system the cause of their poverty. This would mean to oppose the trends of the 20th century with the trends and categories of the 19th century. This would be a goal doomed beforehand to failure.'

'It is natural that socialist development (primarily the present development of socialism under the enormously difficult conditions of inherited backwardness, capitalist surrounding, intrusions and provocations) is not a pleasure trip. It has occurred during the struggle against yesterday's reactionary forces and there does not exist any preceding example for it. It is, therefore, enormously complicated and also burdened with errors and mistakes for the same reason. He who does not want to deceive himself, must learn to look without prejudice, to distinguish incidental and superficial phenomena from lawful and substantial ones, external features, which are incompatible with socialism, from what is peculiar to it. He must appreciate the immense fundamentality of the October Socialist Revolution, which adjudged total freedom of self-determination to all nations and nationalities up to the separation and creation of independent states. He must acknowledge the union of Soviet Republics as possessing absolutely equal rights. He cannot neglect the immense, astonishing prosperity of once backward nations of Russia. He cannot help seeing the gradual, patient, systematic building up of principally new relations between the nations and countries of real socialism.'

'The international nature of socialism has already manifested itself in the past, i.e. by the creation of the Soviet Union. So far one has not understood properly enough that not a renewal of the old Russia, which broke down after World War I, but an entirely new act of the first socialist integration, typical for socialism, was concerned. Under the conditions of World War I this integration could quickly attain state-political integration and or initiate it.'

'The process of socialist integration spreads nowadays to other socialist countries, which have already overcome their backwardness in the main, which have exhausted the possibilities of mere national development to a considerable extent and have to link their further development with a broader and deeper international co-operation. With regard to the conditions created during World War II and later, this new or further process of socialist integration begins with the economy, and it is more or less restricted to it. It is, however, clear that one day it will go and will have to go further.'

'The process of socialist integration (the creation of the USSR, the present integration of the countries of the Council of Mutual Economic Assistance) does not abolish national and state sovereignty. In the USSR there exist not only federal national republics whose sovereignty is expressed in the constitution including the right to unilateral secession from the union, but also each nation and nationality, living to a certain degree compactly, be it small or big, has its form of state rights and sovereignty – from the autonomous national republics to the autonomous national regions and up to the national spheres. The countries of the CMEA preserve the classical, inherited state autonomy, independence and sovereignty. In the present period of the development of national and state sovereignty of socialist countries and nations it does not disappear; on the contrary, it is strengthened. The present socialist integration is not yet a form of supranationality, neither within the framework of unity of the countries of the CMEA nor within the framework of the USSR of other multinational socialist countries. It is a form of internationality. This is not a question of formulation, this is a very substantial difference. Internationality means the preservation and respecting of the national, inclusive sovereignty. It is only a union of different nations and countries, stressing their unity and accentuating the fact that each of them needs the others for its development, that these countries support one another, that they care not only for their own, but also for common interests, that they harmonize their national interests with those of the whole, that they place these interests of the whole – in conformity with the historically necessary trend – before and over their own, specifically national interests. The common, the international, is not alien to the national in this case, it is not separated from it, in a certain sense it is composed of individual national parts, which participate in it. In comparison with immediate and momentary, specifically national, interests the interests of the international socialist whole represent prospective and permanent interests of all nations of the socialist community.'

'However, the Marxists and communists have always been sure (on

the basis of an analogy with the past development, and on the basis of
an analysis of the existing trends of development), that the nation, the
national, is a historical category, which will cease to exist, which will
fade away after its origin and development. The real overcoming of
the national cannot, however, be reached by force, but – on the
contrary – by creating conditions, in order to develop, to exhaust the
possibilities and accede naturally to higher forms. Then this process
will not meet with the aversion of the people, but – on the contrary –
with their support; they will learn from their own experience that
the overcoming, abandoning, giving up of the national will not
impoverish them, but – quite the reverse – enrich them immensely.'

'National sovereignty is, therefore, not an obstacle to peace and the
less so a cause of wars and conflicts. Its overcoming is not, therefore,
a condition of peace as well. National sovereignty is the right of every
nation, a condition of its development. It cannot be removed for
good artificially, even less so by force. It can only fade away naturally
after having exhausted all its possibilities.'

'The real supranational integration is only a question of the future.
Contemporary international integrations differ substantially one from
another. Integration on the capitalist basis always carries in itself the
diseases of the capitalist social order. It is not a real international
integration and it does not lead, it cannot lead to a real, natural overcoming of nationality by internationality. It is not only an endeavour
at maintaining the obsolete capitalist relations, which are always
more dangerous for humanity, but simultaneously also an instrument of the nationalism of the strongest countries and/or their
capitalist monopolies, directed to controlling the world. Its way is not,
therefore, a way of peace, on the one hand; on the other, it is an
organic part of war danger in the contemporary world and in the
present period, and it can even appear as a relatively very independent factor of war danger.'

'Socialist integration, even though it has just been initiated, shows
the real way from nationality to progressive internationality. However, it does not yet exclude national sovereignty, but presupposes it.
It would not be also right to speak about it as a condition of peace in
the world.'

Herbert J. Spiro

Interdependence: A Third Option between Sovereignty and Supranational Integration

DOES EITHER NATIONAL SOVEREIGNTY OR SUPRANATIONAL integration offer the world a pathway to peace? Positing the question in these alternatives seems to rest upon the following analogy: the establishment of national sovereignty occurred at the same time as the national integration, i.e. the 'making whole' of previously un-integrated societies. In the prior condition, before establishment of the national whole, internecine quarrels prevailed rather than peace. Sovereignty and national integration were the parallel pathways to domestic tranquillity and peace. Similarly in the international sphere today, the many competing national sovereignties present obstacles to peace or, worse, constitute the cause of wars, and supranational integration is therefore the pathway to peace.

A FALSE ANALOGY

The analogy is false, for a number of reasons. The sub-units which were integrated into larger national wholes in the course of the establishment of sovereignties were historically pre-sovereign or, at best, proto-sovereign. The sovereignties that would have to be supranationally integrated today are either 'true' sovereignties or, in the vast majority of cases, post-sovereignties. The problems en-countered by integrators in the 17th or 18th centuries, on the one hand, and in the 20th century on the other, are, therefore, qualita-tively different. Moreover, there was a varied range of problems for different founders of national sovereignty even in the earlier period. In the typical continental case, absolutist rulers integrated a new nation from the centre, from above, and by force. However, the need for centralization, the distance between 'above' and 'below', the incidence of force, as well as the coincidence of these processes with one another (i.e. the particular sequence and the degree of their synchronization), varied widely, even on the continent. In Great Britain, yet another pattern was followed, because of the relatively early extension of the run of the royal writ in England and Wales, the sequential and separate settlements of the religious and constitutional issues in the 16th and 17th centuries, the union of the English and Scottish kingdoms thereafter, and the historic first occurrence of an industrial revolution. Neither the typical continental, nor the British case of national integration, seems analogous to any actual or potential supranational integration that is being accomplished or achieved in the present period. *Global* supranational integration of existing states seems impossible and does not even have many advocates. And the kind of *regional* integration that is said to be taking place among the members of the European Community shows no parallels to the continental patterns of national integration which established sovereignty.

There is a third pattern of so-called national integration which has often been held up by advocates of supranational integration, whether their target is a region, like Western Europe, or world government. This model is the United States of America, as represented by its motto, *e pluribus unum*. The perception of American political development from the beginnings of the thirteen separate colonies to full national integration is so simple and elegant, and has been accepted so widely, that I need not describe it here. This perception also happens to be wrong.

The 'integration' of the American polity did not proceed from a centre, was not pushed from above, and was not obtained by force (though its wholeness was challenged and preserved by force in the Civil War). What happened instead in the United States was very different from the prevailing model. By a process which is continuing today, interdependence and, equally important, consciousness of interdependence, has been growing. Regions of the country and both horizontal and vertical groupings of the people have become increasingly aware of their complex, mutual dependence upon one another. Moreover, this awareness has had and continues to have a variety of qualities and manifestations. It is, in a sense, both conscious and unconscious consciousness – if I may be permitted this distinction and the apparent redundancy, as well as the apparent *contradictio in adiecto.* Conscious awareness of interdependence is expressed by politicians, businessmen, educators, and others, including the common man, when they speak of the direct or the mediated effects of their actions upon others, and of their expectation that the reactions of these others will in turn, directly or indirectly, affect themselves. Unconscious consciousness of interdependence manifests itself through behaviour from which we can reasonably infer that it has been undertaken in an 'internalized' kind of awareness of the probability of its repercussive effects upon oneself, which will be transmitted through the various overlapping networks of the polity, of which one perceives oneself as a *more or less* integral component part.

NATIONAL SOVEREIGNTY AND INTEGRATION

I need not reiterate that the political development of the United States has rarely if ever been described, much less analysed, along these lines. But I would like to ask *why* it has been described and explained in the conventional terms criticized above. There are, I think, two convergent answers to this question, one related to older concepts and theories of sovereignty, the other to more recent concepts and theories of integration. 'We, the People of the United States of America' declared independence from Great Britain at the precise time when the doctrine of sovereignty was coming fully into its own in Europe – even though English-speaking practice, as distinguished from the writings of certain English political theorists, accorded much less importance to sovereignty than did continental European practice. As a result, the constitutional Founding Fathers had to address themselves to the problems raised by sovereignty at the same time that they were designing the framework for the first constitutional democracy, a political concept which is – as Carl J. Friedrich made clear to us long ago – incompatible with the concept of sovereignty. In consequence, much of the writing on American political development, especially by otherwise perceptive continental European interpreters, took it for granted that the thirteen separate sovereignties of the original states, with the gradual addition of others, were integrated into the new, whole sovereignty, the entity of the United States of America. For purposes of international law, this understanding may have been accurate enough, but that is irrelevant to our consideration of the historical analogy between national and supranational integration as pathways, respectively, to domestic and global peace. Our question, rather, must be whether a single, 'clear' sovereign on the European continental model was established in the United States and, if so, whether this was the prime cause of domestic tranquillity. My answer is that, far from establishing the European, substantive type of sovereign, the constitution provided the procedural framework for the operation of the 'constituent power', to use Friedrich's term. A political science preoccupied with 'rule' in the sense of *Herrschaft*, and uninterested in politics as the process by which a community deals with the problems it recognizes, failed, with few exceptions, to see this. It is certain, in any case, that internal peace was not imposed upon the expanding United States from the 'centre' of Washington, from above, or by force. On the contrary, the major instance of American behaviour along European or quasi-European lines, in this sense, is associated with the Civil War, of which more later.

The second explanation for conventional *mis*interpretations of American political development is related to more recent theories of 'national integration', that have grown up together with the extensive literature about the so-called 'developing areas'. This approach to the problems of these regions – to put it very briefly and at the expense of some simplification – offers both description and prescription. Events in the developing countries are *de*scribed as moving towards the integration, and frequently the creation, of 'new nations'. Authors of this persuasion also *pre*scribe the goal of national integration as the proper be-all and end-all for the peoples and leaders of the newly independent states of Asia, Africa, and other 'less developed' areas.

The 'national integration' model of American political development is evidently based upon a mechanical analogy with the 'sovereignty' model, especially in its normative dimension which exhorts contemporary developing countries, in effect, to copy the United States as 'the first new nation'. The two models reinforce each other mechanically or negatively, rather than dialectically, thereby clouding our understanding, rather than enhancing it. By the same token, their combined impact is negative also when the attempt is made to apply these models to the problem of pathways to global peace today. If the United States were either as sovereign or as integrated nationally as it should be if the concepts were valid, then supranational integration would have to proceed without the United States. Indeed, if each of the member states of the European Community were as nationally integrated as the theories of national integration would have us believe, then supranational integration at the Communtiy level would prove impossible. One way out of this apparent conceptual dilemma – conceptual in the sense that *something* supra-'national' has evidently been going on in the real world of Western Europe – is to explore possible alternatives to the descriptive aspects of the concept of integration.

TYPES OF INTERDEPENDENCE

The concept of interdependence can provide such an alternative for both the contemporary international and the historical American cases of political development. Indeed, it is through resolution of some of the perplexities raised by the inadequate results of efforts to interpret contemporary international and supranational trends with the aid of conventional concepts like sovereignty and integration, that we can gain a better perspective upon, and more satisfying interpretations of, the past. But neither task is easy, in the face of the pervasiveness – the virtual tyranny – of the dominant concepts, even though much more intellectual, i.e. academic, including academic institutional – capital has been invested in them than political, not to speak of financial, capital. Political analysts have been much louder than political actors in espousing either national or supranational integration. Politicians sense from their experience that they are not engaged in integration and that, if they were, they would be unlikely to succeed. Nevertheless, the analysts may have done substantial harm through propagation of the concept, because of the process of oscillation, between excessive expectations and excessive disappointment, which it can set off among people who live in an intellectual magnetic field whose plus and minus poles are believed to be integration and sovereignty.

The influence of sovereignty, integration, and associated concepts has been so pervasive in interpretations of American political development, that I almost feel we need to lift ourselves up by our conceptual bootstraps in order to view this history as the expansion of consciousness of interdependence. To begin with, because interdependence occurs in the contemporary literature almost exclusively as a concept auxiliary to elaborations of integration, most of the extant material on phenomena of interdependence is loaded in the wrong direction, tempting us to mistake causes for effects. But even at the level of description and classification, we have to start virtually from scratch. We are trying to understand consciousness of degrees of interdependence and we therefore have to ask very simply first how interdependence can be perceived by those who are conscious of it.

Interdependence can be seen as existing and operating in a variety of ways, among a range of participants in a political system, whether national, subnational, or international. Two participants – either individuals or groupings whose members have consciousness of a relevant affinity with one another – may be directly interdependent; A depends upon B for Need 1, and B depends upon A for Need 2. Two participants can be indirectly interdependent; A depends upon C for Good 3, C depends upon B for Good 4, and B depends upon A for Good 5. Interdependence can vary with respect to the *number* of entities perceiving themselves as interdependent. It can vary also with respect to perceptions of *duration* and *intensity* of the relationship, the *volume* of intercourse, and along a spectrum whose extremes are *simplicity*, and *complexity*. Complex interdependence can involve various members of a network *repetitively* in its interactions only, or non-repetitively in several *overlapping* networks. These may *criss-cross* more or less. They may be *tight* or *loose*. Interdependence may be *positive*, as in the division of labour, or *negative*, as in nuclear deterrence. Interdependence varies also of course with regard to the *substance* of the 'goods' involved in the relationship, from labour, flows of communications, travel and migration, and other human goods, through commodities and other economic goods, to hostile, warring, or mutually supportive weapons systems. The formal and informal, more or less institutionalized *procedures* by means of which interdependence is articulated and generally processed constitute another variant of interdependence. In this sense, elections and a national legislature like the Congress or an international organization like the United Nations can be likened to a visible electronic aid to one's understanding of shifting perceptions of patterns of interdependence.

If we could elaborate, refine, and apply in quantitatively and qualitatively comparable ways these and other categories – a formidable task for political science – we should be able to arrive at revised interpretations of phenomena like those conventionally described as the establishment of American sovereignty and the national integration of the United States, or the supranational integration of the members of the European Community. For example, American political development up to the Civil War would appear as the growth of awareness of increasingly complex patterns of interdependence among various regions of the country and sections of the economy and society. During the period of the American Revolution, feelings of interdependence were heightened by the desire to overcome dependence upon Great Britain and the consequent sense that, 'if we do not hang together, we will assuredly all hang separately'. It was the essence of the compromises worked out in the Constitutional Convention that these patterns of domestic interdependence were not, and were not likely to remain, constant and fixed, across the board, but rather fluid, shifting, and issue-specific. One day's allies on one issue could anticipate that they would be tomorrow's antagonists on another. Victory on any one play was therefore considered less important by them than the availability of stable, flexible, efficient, and reliable procedures, or rules of the game, which would protect each participant over the long run, whether he was a temporary loser or a temporary winner. Moreover, these rules had to be and to appear to be generally just and fair, and they had to make the whole complex process plausible and comprehensible to ordinary citizens. This need for procedural reliability and plausibility is clearly reflected in the procedural – or, the non-substantive – character of the constitution itself.

The evolution of the American political system until it was torn by the single great cleavage which led to the Civil War, cannot be accurately described as a course of cumulative centralization from above and by force. On the contrary, and as in other analogous sequences in history, it was two parallel processes – first, the increasing 'complexification' of interdependence of the system as a whole, which led one section, the South, to perceive its own problems as ever more irrelevant and peripheral to the rest of the country, and second, the emergence of the single dominant issue of slavery between South and North – which led to the 'rebellion'. People in the South no longer felt that they were so enmeshed in the many evolving patterns of complex interdependence of the political system, that they would stand to lose more from secession and its break-up than from its continued existence along with their own increasing marginality in it. In this instance, the effects on awareness of the facts of interdependence were less than would have been the case without the geographical contiguity of those who sensed their own marginality so keenly that they were willing to concentrate entirely upon the single most important issue, to the exclusion of all the 'lesser' networks of interdependence in which they also participated.

The Civil War was settled by means which, in the conventional categories, look like the reimposition of national sovereignty, so that national reintegration appeared to have provided the pathway to the re-establishment of domestic peace. In any event, the subsequent history of the United States can be taken as a classic model of the expansion of popular consciousness, of the proliferation of mountingly complex, overlapping, criss-crossing, and shifting networks of interdependence, within a procedural framework sufficiently resilient to make its own operation appear to be in the continuous overwhelming interest of almost all the participants: *almost* but not quite all, because the increasing tightness and complexity of interdependence from time to time led some groups to perceive their own situation as so peripheral to the interests of the 'rationally' enmeshed others, and/or led these groups to perceive the very complexity of the total nexus as beyond comprehension and therefore also beyond exploitation in their own interests, that they did one or both of two things: they tried to opt out into desperate quietism, or they tried to attack the system by various kinds of 'blackmail', e.g. strikes by technologically obsolescent labour unions, diffuse violence by members of a hopeless urban 'underclass', the occupation of government buildings by ethnic groups left behind, or violence directed against points of high real or symbolic interdependence like passenger aircraft and government officials. Apart from marginal groups, however, the awareness of interdependence, both conscious and unconscious, is so strong, that it inhibits all others from resolute efforts to transform or to destroy the system of interdependence itself, no matter how alienated, disaffected, or embittered they may be over economic, constitutional, generational, foreign policy, or other issues.

INHIBITIVE INTERDEPENDENCE AND A
DIALECTICAL EXCURSION

The inhibitive effects of popular consciousness of complex interdependence can also provide a powerful explanation for a phenomenon – or rather, the absence of a phenomenon – which has puzzled many historians and political scientists, especially critical students of the Marxian philosophy of history. According to this philosophy, proletarian revolutions were most likely to occur in the most advanced capitalist, bourgeois, industrialized societies. However, in neither the last nor the present century, has successful – or even unsuccessful – revolutionary class warfare occurred in any of the industrialized societies for which Marx did, or would have, predicted it. Instead, the great Marxist-Communist revolutions took place in Russia and China, both relatively unindustrialized at the time, backward, agrarian, and without a sizeable industrial proletariat. We have an interesting literature that seeks to explain these facts, e.g. Adam Ulam's suggestion that communism is useful both to instil the functional equivalent of the 'discipline of the machine process' in peasant masses and to provide them with an elaborate promise of a better future in order to elicit greater current self-sacrifice and self-denial. The concept of interdependence seems to provide a better explanation, particularly when we combine it with a reformulation of the Marxian dialectic, which can be drawn from interdependence itself. But this requires an excursion into Marxian dialectics.

According to Marx and Engels, history is kept moving by contradictions in the material conditions of human existence. Most important under capitalism is the irreconcilable contradiction between the social mode of production and the private mode of appropriation, which subsumes distribution and consumption. In recent decades, the mode of production has undergone profound change: the discovery of new sources of energy (power) like uranium, nuclear technology, automation, the development of communications and transportation technology, including the transportation of power like liquified natural gas. The transportation of power, incidentally, involves both production *and* distribution. It therefore suggests that we can no longer draw a clear boundary line between these two human activities, so that the 'real' dialectical contradiction should be sought elsewhere. Distribution in the Marxian sense has in fact by now been largely socialized in the non-Marxist sense, through national and multinational corporations, credit cards, car and equipment rentals, and so forth. Of course, to say that distribution has been socialized does not mean that 'appropriation' has been equalized, but rather that it is subject to centralized, 'network-interdependent' co-ordination. This in turn is not necessarily the same as central planning and control, but rather a system of complex, overlapping, criss-crossing, shifting patterns of interdependence.

Marx was preoccupied with increasing production – hence his conviction that it would be permanently impossible to abolish child labour. The United States and other developed countries, including the Soviet Union, have achieved levels of productivity beyond his wildest dreams. The contradictions which Marx saw within capitalist societies, according to some interpretations, have been raised to the 'higher' level of conflicts between developed and less developed countries and regions. The enormous productivity of the developed industrial economies constantly increases their need for labour and raw materials, both of which are to be found in greatest abundance in the less developed countries. The developed countries compete among themselves for labour and raw materials, and especially for the resources required for energy production. As a result, networks of interdependence, both among the developed countries, and between them and the less developed countries, are becoming tighter and ever more complex. This interdependence, and the dialectically growing awareness of it, may under certain conditions have an inhibiting effect upon attempts to resolve by means of violence any particular set of contradictions.

PRODUCTION VERSUS DESTRUCTION

But there is another inhibiting factor at work, which has until now been even more effective than interdependence in preventing direct violence between the greatest powers. This is the tremendous growth in the means of destruction. Marx posited the mode of appropriation as the dialectical antithesis of the mode of production, probably because the contradictions between ever more social production and ostentatiously private appropriation and consumption appeared to be the most obvious and self-evident of contradictions in the mid-19th century. However, the logical antithesis of production is destruction – and if the dialectical method is anything it is a method of logic. Perhaps, if Marx were alive today, he would find that in today's material conditions of human existence, where production and distribution can no longer be objectively distinguished from one another, the most contradictory material dialectic is the one which operates between the thesis of the mode of production-cum-distribution and the antithesis of the mode of destruction. This must be understood as comprising not only global weapons systems, but also depletion of natural resources and destruction of the environment. At the same time that unprecedented productivity has led to the emergence of the new patterns of international interdependence mentioned above, its dialectical opposite, unprecedented destructiveness, is creating higher levels of consciousness of negative interdependence, particularly among the nuclear super-powers, but also among all peoples, as shown, for example, by the Stockholm Conference on the Environment and by efforts to regulate exploitation of the seabeds.

Marx advocated the socialization of the means of production. Given today's changed material conditions of existence, he might advocate, as the contemporary equivalent of that socialization, the conscious global organization of interdependence for the purpose of raising levels of awareness of the new mode of destruction. Marx opposed the private, individual, non-social, and uncentralized mode of appropriation/distribution in the 1860s. Similarly, if he were alive today, Marx might oppose the national or regional compartmentalized independent or dependent use of presently available means of destruction in more or less localized wars; refusal to participate in world politics through self-isolation; and belief in the feasibility of establishing and maintaining in practice a distinction between the use of tactical and strategic nuclear weapons. Late in his life, Marx became ambivalent about the need for or the likelihood of a violent revolution. His communist heirs have also wavered on this issue, as for example Lenin with respect to 'peaceful coexistence' and the present-day Soviet rulers in their evolving interpretation of that concept. In any case, they have accepted – as, from a purely theoretical point of view, they have to accept – the ultimate destructiveness of nuclear weapons as an objective factor in the material conditions of existence.

For Marx, recognition of the objective realities of the mode of production generated higher levels of consciousness, i.e. in the 19th century, of proletarian class consciousness, and thereby shaped the course of history. In our own time, the mode of destruction and recognition of its objective realities (in the Marxian sense) 'necessarily' performs this same function of raising consciousness of common interests among ever larger numbers of human beings. Globally, there seems to be less awareness of the positive benefits of productive interdependence than of the negative perils of destructive interdependence. (There may be a parallel here to the evolution of individual rights under the English Common Law – by contrast with the Roman Civil Law – generally formulated and understood as prohibitions upon government against committing specific acts *vis-à-vis* its subjects/citizens, instead of being formulated and understood as positive rights, the enjoyment of which is guaranteed to citizens by their government.) Often, growth in consciousness of positive benefits has had the effect of restricting rather than widening the circle of those who believed themselves to have common interests – witness Lenin's fulminations against mere 'trade union consciousness'. The main beneficiaries of productive interdependence are generally in a good strategic position to manipulate consciousness of it in their own narrower behalf. On the other hand, the consequences of the contemporary mode of destruction are too universally evident to be easily susceptible to this kind of manipulation on behalf of less than universal interests. For example, developed and less developed countries operate on the basis of different and antagonistic forms of consciousness of productive interdependence. But their awareness, at least their 'generalized' awareness, of the risks inherent in destructive interdependence is much more similar, if not identical. Of course, consciousness of the benefits of productive interdependence and of the dangers of destructive interdependence move in direct dialectical relation to one another, and the function of thesis or antithesis may be performed by either. Nuclear energy was first unlocked to destroy targets, then to produce power. The synthesis of contradictions between the mode of production and the mode of destruction takes place in consciousness of interdependence, which views the possibilities of the human future in terms *either* expansive, progressive, and global, *or* restrictive, regressive, and isolationist.

The preceding analysis has been cast in terms of the international dialectic between production and destruction, because some interpreters of Marxism hold that the domestic class conflict which Marx saw in the most advanced capitalist societies of his time has now been raised to the level of international class conflict between – broadly speaking – developed and less developed countries. It is conceivable, however, that if Marx had focused upon production-destruction, instead of production-appropriation, he would have arrived at conclusions about the history of the capitalist societies which he studied analogous to those at which we can arrive in our study of international society.

CONSCIOUSNESS OF INTERDEPENDENCE AND VIOLENCE

If Marx had focused upon the dialectic between production and destruction and the enhancement in popular consciousness of interdependence to which it is likely to lead, he might have predicted that Great Britain was the least likely country to experience a proletarian revolution in the 19th century. Marx and Engels based much of their analysis and their theory upon the land of the first Industrial Revolution, where they spent their own most productive years, exploiting the wealth of economic and social data available in the Reading Room of the British Museum and elsewhere. We may conjecture today that their own comparative observations might have suggested to them that the British people had reached a higher level of consciousness of both productive and destructive interdependence than any of the continental peoples of the time, or the people of the United States, *circa* 1867, when *Das Kapital* was published. Of course, objective conditions and subjective consciousness of these conditions do not always coincide. Nevertheless, it seems reasonable on the evidence to assert that domestic productive and domestic destructive interdependence were further advanced in Britain than elsewhere. This had the consequence of making potential revolutionary leaders and their followers aware of both the actual benefits which they were enjoying from productive interdependence, and the risks they would be taking by unleashing major destructive power within the web of interdependence, through either revolution or reaction. Potential revolutionaries were inhibited from launching a real revolution, because the present benefits of industrialization, including acquisition of the empire, seemed more obvious than the possible benefits of working-class rule; *and* because the dangers to themselves, along with everyone else within the complexities of domestic interdependence, of the use of available destructive power seemed also greater and more obvious than the possible benefits of conceivable arrangements *après le déluge*.

In this sense, consciousness of productive and destructive interdependence reduces commitment to revolutionary goals and, as recent history has shown, such commitment is at least as important a prerequisite to revolutionary action as actual material wherewithal and strategic opportunities. In contemporary advanced industrial societies, the working or other revolutionary class – nowadays it would include intellectuals, students, 'youth', certain ethnic minorities, and other marginal groups – probably has a higher degree of awareness of productive and destructive interdependence than any other class, with the possible exceptions of top politicians and administrators and top corporate management. This again inhibits the commitment of this class to genuinely revolutionary goals. The so-called 'events' of May 1968 in France provide a nice illustration; throughout the general strike in May and early June no Paris restaurants closed down, nor did they suffer food shortages, because the same high quality produce continued to be trucked in from the provinces – and all this despite the petrol delivery strike.

In today's advanced industrial polities – and they should be referred to as polities rather than societies, economies, or cultures, because the 'boundaries' between these compartments of existence are much less concretely visible than between the equivalent sectors of less developed countries – the means of destruction available to both the state and also to 'private' non-state or anti-state movements are very great indeed. Their destructiveness parallels that of nuclear weapons in the international system. In contemporary developed countries, awareness of the potentially total destructiveness of domestic organized means of violence is so high, that no class movement is capable of marshalling a positive commitment to the use of massive violence on behalf of its own class interests which is stronger than its negative commitment against the use of these means of destruction employed in the course of an internal revolution. The proof of this hypothesis lies in the fact that no revolutions have occurred in developed countries. The last European countries to have had civil wars are Spain and Greece, which were among Western Europe's most backward countries at the time. Revolutions on the Marxist or counter-Marxist model have occurred only in less developed countries, where consciousness of interdependence does not extend beyond very narrow horizons, precisely because the available means of destruction are not risky and revolutionary leaders and followers can realistically hope to achieve their own goals without fear of a self- or class-defeating total national disaster. On the level of contemporary world politics, the same has been true of less developed regions, and it is for these reasons that the industrialized states – and more especially the super-powers with their highest level of destructive interdependence – seem in effect to be operating upon a tacit understanding (of the facts, not of each other) which declares regional wars and national liberation struggles to be peripheral, tries to place them in separate compartments, and refuses to let them be escalated to the global, nuclear, super-power level. These circumstances also explain why especially the super-powers have shown greater concern than the less developed countries for the need to develop a lasting consensus on the still evolving, genuinely new procedures for global intercourse (not merely for international diplomacy). Some less developed countries still pursue specific substantive goals and victories and, with their more limited awareness of global destructive interdependence, they do not sense the same urgent need to adapt traditional procedures of both domestic and international intercourse to the new mode of destruction.

In both national and international politics, there is one apparent exception to this thesis about consciousness of productive and destructive interdependence, which actually proves the rule: individuals and groups who exploit a high awareness of interdependence for their own criminal or other purely selfish or negative purposes, like aircraft highjackers, kidnappers of diplomats, strikers in key industries, small ethnic or religious minorities, etc. Such groups are made aware of their capacity to blackmail the rest of the population because the growing complexity of the expanding larger patterns of interdependence is about to make them marginal or redundant. So they lash out in desperation and in ways often reminiscent of the original *saboteurs* try – ultimately always without success – to hold up society before their particular simple social or economic function has become obsolete; e.g. stevedores in the face of containerization, or Ulster Protestants before the historic problem of the Irish is eventually *aufgehoben* in the larger Europe. Their desperation drives them to a belated recognition of their own role in the older, simpler pattern of interdependence which is about to be superseded by a more complex one. Palestinian Liberation Organization terrorists blow up Swiss, Belgian, and US planes, and murder diplomats and Olympic athletes, in order to exploit a kind of interdependence temporarily manufactured by themselves in a world which, as they perceive it, has relegated their problems to the periphery because it takes a more sophisticated view of the objective mode of destruction on a global scale. But – and herein lies the tragedy of the marginal men and the hope for mankind – these desperate acts dialectically raise the general awareness of global interdependence brought about by contradictions between the modes of production and destruction, by driving home the need for corrective action – action, that is, to structure interdependence and consciousness of it creatively, so as to promote the kind of procedural consensus which will be capable of containing destructiveness and of using productivity for the benefit of all.

MISSED OPPORTUNITIES TO INTEGRATE

Whatever purposes national sovereignty may have served in its heyday, its continued existence today clearly presents no pathway to peace. Indeed, only the rulers of a few less developed countries can conduct themselves like old-fashioned sovereigns in their foreign relations, and do so regardless of the degree of national integration of their subjects, precisely because of their marginality to the global networks of interdependence. But simply because national sovereignty presents no pathway to peace we need not jump to the conclusion that supranational integration does.

It is sometimes argued that the erosion of national sovereignty which has been brought about by the growth of positive and negative interdependence will facilitate supranational integration, if indeed it will not make integration inevitable. Technology has made national boundaries porous and permeable. The threat of nuclear war has led to the organization of great alliances, whose members have surrendered certain ingredients of conventional sovereignty to supranational or international bodies. Economic interdependence, at least among the capitalist countries, is so highly developed, that none of them could follow a policy of autarky even if it wanted to, and none of them does. As a result, the major powers, which presumably present the greatest threat to peace, should properly be regarded as post-sovereignties. These, the argument concludes, could be more easily integrated than true sovereignties into new supranational entities.

If this line of reasoning were correct, then the height of the cold war would have presented the best opportunities for supranational integration within each of the two contending blocs. The Soviet Union was supreme within the communist bloc, and its satellites behaved the way satellites should. The United States was the un-disputed leader of its camp, whose other members, while less dependent upon Washington than the satellites were upon Moscow, were dependants and in some instances clients in the true sense of the term. International behaviour was highly predictable. West and East normally disagreed with each other across the board, e.g. at the United Nations, and on the rare occasions when they agreed – as on the 'package' admission of new members to the UN – they did so also across the board on each side. Both the Soviet Union and the United States should have had splendid opportunities during the years of the cold war to integrate their respective camps hege-monially into entities designed to become 'supranations', at least ultimately. We know the reasons, different, on each side, why this did not happen. More interesting for our discussion is the unlikeli-hood that such supranational integration would have shown the way to peace between the two camps or, for that matter, within each.

A paradox arises here, but only if we examine these facts in the light of the conventional supposition, based upon the mistaken analogy between national and supranational integration, that expansive integration leads to peace. The logical opposite of this supposition must be that lack of integration – i.e. lack of 'wholeness' – or worse, the relative disintegration of something that was more integrated before, should lead to war. The reverse, however, seems to have been happening during the last few years, as we have moved away from the cold war, away from containment and towards engagement, away from confrontation and towards negotiation and co-operation. Both the communist world and the anti-communist world, and also those who identify themselves as non-aligned states, are less integrated than each group was ten or fifteen years ago. Yet there seem to be fewer dangers of war and better chances for peace. But things have this appearance neither because of intra-bloc integration, nor because of any supranational integration transcending the old cleavage of the cold war, whether within one region like Europe, or globally as in the United Nations.

INHIBITIVE INTERDEPENDENCE

What happened instead of intra-bloc or supra-bloc integration was the gradual proliferation and expansion of ever more complex, kaleidoscopically shifting networks of interdependence, along with the expansion of popular and elite consciousness of this proliferation and expansion. While the apparent integrative trends in the Soviet and the Western blocs were decelerated or reversed, member states of, and other entities within, each of them developed a variety of new relationships with old and new partners. Novel types of participants in world politics, like multinational corporations, became increasingly involved in what someone has called 'the multinational game', which should more appropriately be labelled the 'interdependence expansion game'. Examples at all levels are innumerable and so well known that they need not be cited here.

To illustrate the way in which interdependence can operate, along with the descriptive and conceptual difficulties which will have to be overcome before scholarship on interdependence can achieve the same apparent clarity which much literature on sovereignty and integration used to convey, we can take a look at the quinquelateral of great centres of power which, in the opinion of some practitioners and students of international politics, are emerging in the world today: the United States, the Soviet Union, Western Europe, Japan, and China. This would be a relatively easy case study of interdependence, because it ignores the rest of the world. Nevertheless, it would be extremely difficult to get even a descriptive handle on the multiplicity of varied relationships of interdependence, and their reflections in popular and elite awareness, among these five. On the other hand, the mere graphic representation of the pentagon can help our understanding. For example, we have heard the beginnings of a debate within the United States about the implications of President Nixon's notion of the five great centres of power for American relations with the two communist giants, on the one hand, and with Western Europe and Japan on the other. Some of the President's critics have expressed the fear that improvement of relations within the US–USSR–China triangle would be accompanied by deterioration, or at least stagnation, of relations within the US–EC–Japan triangle. In fact, there are and will continue to be large differences between our relations with our allies in Europe and Japan and our association with Moscow and Peking. The diagram shows, *inter alia*, that the United States is involved in both triangles and that it is the only one of the five to be so involved, in what might be called the 'mutual destruction' or the 'potentially destructive' triangle and the 'capitalist' or the 'superproductive' triangle. The fact that the United States is the only power to be involved in these two triangles – in terms of the global dialectic of production-destruction, they are the most important of the ten triangles in the pentagon – shows, incidentally, that inferences of quantitative or qualitative equality among the five centres are erroneous. The point about quinquelateralism is not that there are five equally powerful centres, which indeed there are not, or that relationships among these centres are equivalent, which they assuredly are not. But there are five major centres which have a variety of relations with one another – in addition to their relations with the rest of the world, which clearly cannot be left out of account – and which, for a variety of reasons, *including* global interdependence among the five, bear special responsibilities for world peace.

The salient facts about a pentagon are simple: it contains ten pairs, ten triangles and five quadrilaterals. In our global pentagon, all of these sets of relationships exist, but each pair differs from every other pair, each triangle differs from every other triangle, and each

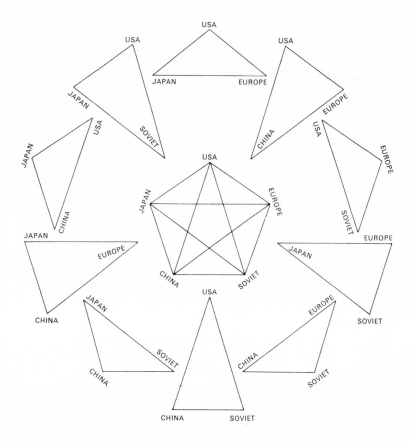

quadrilateral differs from every other quadrilateral – in all respects: kinds of relations, their volume, continuity of flow, subjective importance accorded to them, and so forth. The diagram is not only abstracted from the rest of the real world – lesser centres of power, less developed countries, international organizations, circumscribed regional international systems, supranational corporations or churches, etc. – but it also has a symmetry which is wholly absent in the real world. A realistic portrayal in graphic and quantifiable terms of quinquelateral relations offers a considerable challenge to imaginative students of world politics. While we are waiting for responses to that challenge, we can use the abstracted symmetrical diagram to enhance our own awareness of the complexities of interdependence.

Each of the five 'centres' is internally centralized to a different degree – from the European Community, sometimes still referred to as a 'headless wonder', at one end of the spectrum, to the highly centralized and non-porous two mutually hostile communist centres at the other end. But decision-makers – including, in the US–EC–Japan triangle, participants in public debates – in all five constantly operate in awareness of the repercussions of their relations with any one (set of) interlocutor(s) upon all the others (or other sets). The United States, in its expanding relations with China and the Soviet Union, has acted in constant awareness of the interdependence between this triangle and the US–EC–Japan triangle. Members of the great Pacific quadrilateral, US–USSR–China–Japan, in adjusting the whole range of co-operative and/or antagonistic relationships, act with varying degrees of awareness of the probable effects upon Europe of these changes, and the consequences of these effects upon bilateral and other relations between Europe and each of them. This is true regardless of the substance of a particular policy, whether it be security, trade, energy, development, cultural exchange, or anything else.

Action in awareness of interdependence in this sense evidently differs from conventional 19th-century balance-of-power politics. The Concert of Europe, as it happens, also involved five powers considered great by the standards of their time. But they were much less heterogeneous than today's emerging centres; they did not face the danger of global destruction presented by nuclear weapons; they could and did divert their energies to extra-European areas where their excursions could on occasion be kept insulated from the Concert itself; they were less aware even of the objectively lower degree of mutual interdependence; and they operated within certain accepted standards of procedural and substantive legitimacy. All of this encouraged and facilitated mechanical power manipulations, especially by the 'outsider' or externally least interdependent power, Great Britain. Today, none of the five centres is an outsider in this sense, because the web of quinquelateral interdependence is being spun ever more finely around the shrinking globe. Moreover, the high degree of mutual interdependence in the US–EC–Japan triangle, and the relative constancy of these relationships, discourages mechanical manipulations.

All of this places unprecedented demands upon diplomacy at a time when, because of the cumulative erosion it suffered during the second world war and the cold war, the consensus on the procedural framework of diplomacy is thin and weak. Meanwhile, substantive agreements are also harder to arrive at than in either the 19th century or the period between the two world wars. In addition, foreign policy is being increasingly exposed to domestic politics, at least in the non-communist world. The conduct of world politics – which is greater than the sum of the foreign policies of all states – therefore increasingly resembles the conduct of domestic politics in a new – indeed, a novel and model-less – constitutional democracy, like the United States in the classic age of the Republic, which has been wrongly called the period of national integration.

International interdependence and awareness of it are obviously growing. Increasing awareness of complex interdependence seems to be having an inhibitive effect upon grossly violent behaviour, especially on the part of the five great centres. Those who govern in each realize that they have so great a stake in the continuation and improvement of the global system, that no probable gains from violent attacks upon other members would justify the risk of its destruction. Like the Founders and other early American politicians, global politicians today face formidable tasks: to make complex interdependence popularly understandable, to keep it from frustrating or driving to desperation potentially marginal groups, to make the new system absorptive and resilient, and to make it work. Above all, they must make interdependence comprehensible and they must continue to elaborate the functional equivalent of a procedural 'constitution'. If complexity passes understanding, those who fail to comprehend that the system is of ultimate benefit to themselves may lash out 'irrationally' at its most exposed parts, which are precisely high points of real or symbolic interdependence. Those who fear that their own problems are given a low position in global priority rankings by the super-powers may try to settle their own regional quarrels in their own violent ways, or to suck one or another of the great powers into conflicts which, viewed *sub specie mundi*, are peripheral.

The work of building a new consensus upon the emerging informal global constitution for the age of interdependence is of supreme importance. As President Nixon has said: 'We can forge a network of relationships and of interdependencies that restrain aggression and that take the profit out of war.' ... 'We can seek a new structure of global relationships in which all nations, friend and adversary, participate and have a stake.'

Donald J. Puchala

Internal Order and Peace: An Integrated Europe in World Affairs

IF POLITICAL AND ECONOMIC ORGANIZATION BEYOND THE NATION-state is to prevail in the future, as it well might, what is to be the nature of relations between and among supranational units or regional blocs? Will such relations buttress or endanger world peace? To such broad questions there are no answers. But to a derivative set of more specific questions, which probe the same kinds of concerns, we can attempt answers. We can ask, and hope to discover, for example, how newly integrated units behave in their external relations, and we can also ask why they behave as they do. From this we can postulate a world of super-units successively entering the international system, and then perhaps say something about the impacts that such entrances are likely to make. While an exercise of this nature could be carried out simply for the sake of expanding theoretical knowledge, it could also be put to very practical and immediate use in lending perspective on the external relations of the European Communities and the impacts of the EEC on world affairs. This last, and most practical concern, is the object of this paper.

There is no question about the fact that European integration, even as far as it has gone, has contributed to world peace.[1] Europe is no longer the internecine battlefield that it was for centuries. The Franco-German border is no longer arrayed with fortresses. Nor is the English Channel still cherished as a barrier to invasion from the continent. Europe has attained internal order and it has prospered

---

[1] Joseph S. Nye Jr., *Peace in Parts*, Little-Brown, Boston, 1971, *passim*. Nye discusses the relationship between regionalism and internal conflict resolution in the context of several cases including the Western European case.

under the peace this has brought. It stands today as a showplace for international co-operation.

Yet this view of European integration and peace, appealing as it is, really is a somewhat restricted view. It considers what European integration has done for intra-European politics, but it passes over what European integration may be doing for global politics. There is, therefore, need for a broader and somewhat more sober assessment of the EEC's role in global affairs.

HOW DO NEWLY INTEGRATED UNITS BEHAVE INTERNATIONALLY?

While the European experience today is in many ways unique, our era is certainly not the first in history during which a new economic or political unit, composed of formerly smaller units, has entered the international system.[2] Indeed, through time international integration has injected many new actors into world politics. Germany, Italy, the United States and Switzerland, for example, are among these. What is most pertinent for the purposes of this analysis is that historical episodes involving the international debuts of newly integrated units reflect a rich variety in patterns of external behaviour.

In some cases, notably during the period of the *Zollverein* in Germany and throughout the early Swiss Confederation, one observes a pattern of *passivity, drift, and fragmentation* in external relations.[3] The units in question encountered great difficulty in finding consensus for their external actions, with the result that common foreign policies were not usually formulated at all. Those that were formulated could not be changed. Collective action was delayed, and it was generally less than effective when finally executed. Such units were also prone to internal crises over external questions, as a result of which, more often than not, different subgroups went their own ways in foreign affairs.[4]

---

[2] See, Karl W. Deutsch, *et al.*, *Political Community and the North Atlantic Area*, Princeton University Press, Princeton, N.J., 1957.

[3] W. O. Henderson, *The Zollverein*, Cambridge University Press, London, 1939, pp. 179–86 and *passim.*; E. Bonjour, H. S. Offler and G. R. Potter, *A Short History of Switzerland*, Clarendon Press, Oxford, 1952, pp. 89 ff.; William Martin, *Switzerland from Roman Times to the Present*, Elek Books, London, 6th ed., 1966, pp. 100 ff.

[4] Henderson, *op. cit.*, pp. 207 ff. and Chap. VIII; Bonjour, Offler and Potter, *op. cit.*, p. 95.

By contrast, a pattern of *rapid, effective, collective initiative and response* is also observable in some cases – in Bismarckian Germany, to be sure, but also in the United States at the turn of the 20th century.[5] In such cases, the newly integrated actors found no great difficulty or strain in acting in unitary fashion in external affairs. But, contrariwise, in some cases, primarily in America between 1870 and 1899, in Italy during roughly the same period, and in Germany under William II, external behaviour reflected patterns of *wavering, erratic initiative and response*.[6] Here actions and reactions were rapid enough, and the units did customarily act in unitary fashion, but there were marked inconsistencies in the styles and substance of international outputs from one issue to the next and sometimes from one week to the next.

Substantively speaking, there is also notable variety in the kinds of policies pursued by different newly integrated units *vis-à-vis* the world around them. These may be given a twofold classification. On the one hand there is an *adaptive* pattern characterized by moderate and prudent initiatives and responses, limited pugnaciousness and competitiveness, intermittent co-operativeness, general respect for the international *status quo*, and general acceptance of the prevailing international hierarchy.[7] On the other hand there is a *disruptive* pattern marked by forceful and adventurous initiatives and responses, intense competitiveness, general disrespect for the international *status quo* and general rejection of the prevailing international hierarchy.[8] As described, these two patterns represent polar extremes, and actual historical experience ranged between them. The Bismarckian system (especially between 1870 and 1880) is perhaps closest to the adaptive pole, whereas the German Empire after 1890

---

[5] A. J. P. Taylor, *The Course of German History*, Methuen, London, 1945, pp. 127–56; Golo Mann, *A History of Germany Since 1789*, Chatto & Windus, London, 1968, *passim.*; Samuel Eliot Morrison, *The Oxford History of the American People*, Oxford Press, London, 1965, Chap. XLIX.

[6] J. W. Pratt, *Expansionists of 1898*, The Johns Hopkins Press, Baltimore, 1936, Chap. I and *passim.*; Morrison, *op. cit.*, Chap. XLVI; Denis Mack Smith, *Italy: A Modern History*, The University of Michigan Press, Ann Arbor, rev. ed., 1969, pp. 103 ff.; Benedetto Croce, *A History of Italy, 1871–1915*, Clarendon Press, Oxford, 1929, pp. 106–25. Note: the United States is considered a newly integrated unit during the period 1870 to 1913 because this was the period of reunification after the American Civil War.

[7] Taylor, *op. cit.*, pp. 107–56; Morrison, *op. cit.*, pp. 816–27.

[8] Taylor, *op. cit.*, pp. 156–96; Mann, *op. cit.*, pp. 244 ff.; Pratt, *op. cit.*, *passim.*; Smith, *op. cit.*, pp. 119 ff.

comes nearest to the disruptive pole. Among other cases, the *Zollverein*, when it acted at all, acted adaptively in economic dealings with other powers of its time, though from about 1854 onward the external bargaining of the *Zollverein* showed increasing obduracy.[9] The United States embarked upon a disruptive course in the 1880s and 1890s, but later acted to buttress international stability. Italy entered the international system with an adaptive attitude in 1870 (save for some ill-feelings towards Austria) but then lapsed into adventurism. The Swiss were thoroughly disruptive for 200 years, only to be perpetually neutralized during the turmoils of the Reformation.[10]

The factors that account for these striking variations in the style and substance of the external behaviour of newly integrated units are all familiar to the student of international relations. They are factors that influence the actions and reactions of all units in international politics. Yet, as will be seen, they affect newly integrated units most acutely, partly because of extraordinarily strong centrifugal forces within such units, and partly because of tensions and uncertainties surrounding the 'newness' of the units and anxieties about their appropriate interests and roles in world affairs.

First, it makes a difference whether or not a newly integrated unit is institutionally equipped to make and execute a foreign policy. By 'institutionally equipped' I mean (a) that practices and procedures exist for finding consensus on questions of external relations with some dispatch, (b) that central authoritative roles exist in the foreign policy realm, and (c) that the unit, as a unit, has instruments available for external use (e.g., such as negotiating authority or military forces). Needless to say that, in historical cases, institutional capability explained much of the difference between patterns of passivity, drift, and fragmentation and those of rapid, effective, collective initiative and response.

Secondly, it makes a difference whether or not a newly integrated unit has a strong central leadership. By this I mean a group of men who identify the unit, who are formally responsible for its external relations, who are endowed with sufficient vision to perceive a role and map a course for the unit in world affairs, and who are politically talented enough to harmonize diverse internal interests and powerful enough to suppress those which cannot be harmonized. If historical

---

[9] Henderson, *op. cit.*, pp. 256 ff.
[10] Martin, *op. cit.*, pp. 100–1.

experience is any guide, strong, gifted central leadership is absolutely essential for stemming the centrifugal tendencies which afflict newly integrated units. It is noteworthy too that, in order to act in world affairs, a newly integrated unit does not necessarily have to have a central elite (or even central institutions or foreign policy procedures). Nor, apparently, does the presence or absence of such leaders and roles make much difference as between adaptive and disruptive external behaviour. The unit does however have to have central mechanisms and leaders if it is to have its own foreign policy. If the newly integrated unit is incapable of making policies of its own, as some are, but is nevertheless acting internationally, as all do, then it is more than likely that the unit is acting out the policies and preferences of some ascendant internal faction. Such factions tend to step into leadership voids to capitalize upon the power and prestige of the new unit and direct its external relations towards the fulfilment of their sub-elite self-interests.[11] Furthermore, when leadership voids exist, but when the balance among internal factions is such that none can remain ascendant for very long, the result can easily be erratic, wavering and generally inconsistent external behaviour as first one and then another faction temporarily seizes central control.

The ends and goals of elites and sub-elites are a third factor of crucial importance in explaining the external behaviour of newly integrated units. While it is certainly not always true that men get what they want from their international pursuits, it must be the case that the ends they seek will be reflected in the style and substance of their behaviour. With regard to newly integrated units, with their special propensity to seizure by ascendant factions, the ends, goals, and interests of such sub-elites tend often to be more directly related to actual external behaviour than are the goals espoused and enunciated by central elites.[12] Goal pursuits, of course, can differentiate between adaptive and disruptive external behaviour.

Fourth, and especially important in the experiences of newly integrated units, are elite perceptions of relative deprivation and rank-disequilibrium *vis-à-vis* the rest of the international system.[13] The elites (or ascendant sub-elites) of such units tend often to be

[11] Henderson, *op. cit.*, Chap. V and *passim*; Taylor, *op. cit.*, pp. 164–6; Morrison, *op. cit.*, Chap. XLV.

[12] Cf., for example, Taylor, *op. cit.*, p. 165.

[13] Johan Galtung, 'A Structural Theory of Aggression', *Journal of Peace Research*, Vol. I, No. 2, 1964, pp. 95–119.

acutely uncertain about exactly where their units ought to fit into the international hierarchy and about the kinds of rewards that ought to be forthcoming from international undertakings. If history is a guide, the predominant tendency among elites of newly integrated units is to expect major power status for their units, to resent those who refuse to accord such status, and to strive generally to revise the international hierarchy.[14] Such tendencies become marked in instances where the units manage to earn high rank in certain dimensions of international accomplishment, but are refused high rank in others. We hear, for example, of 'economic giants and political dwarfs', and we expect that such economic giants will eventually strive to become political giants too, and perhaps military and cultural giants as well. In general, we might expect that the elites of newly integrated units will be more likely than not to go about accumulating symbols of 'great powerness' until their anxieties about relative deprivation and rank-disequilibrium subside.[15] The presence, absence or greater or lesser intensity of such anxieties sometimes makes the difference between adaptiveness and disruptiveness in external relations.

Fifth, and finally, the prevailing style and ethos in the international system certainly affect the behaviour of new actors entering into it. Most international actors tend to do unto others what others do unto them, and newly integrated actors behave no differently. This point need not be laboured, though it is very important. New actors are more likely than not to play the international political and economic game in the way it is being played at the time of their debut. If it is a competitive and aggressive game, new players may well be as competitive and aggressive as the old hands, and perhaps a bit more so as to dramatize their upstart status. If, on the other hand, the game is a conciliatory and co-operative one, new players might well be expected to adapt to the pacific rules.

Five factors then – institutional structure, leadership, elite aspirations, elite perceptions of status and the character of the international environment, have, historically at least, accounted for much of the variation in the external behaviour of newly integrated units. However, many of the relationships between these factors and behavioural patterns had to be discussed in the conditional because none of these linkages are bivariate. Indeed, it is really the five

[14] Croce, *op. cit.*, pp. 106–9; Smith, *op. cit.*, p. 119; Taylor, *op. cit.*, pp. 152 and 167–75; Morrison, *op. cit.*, p. 800.

[15] Taylor, *op. cit.*, p. 152; Morrison, *op. cit.*, p. 823.

factors in combination that explain and differentiate among patterns of external behaviour among newly integrated units. Some reinforce the effects of others; while some cancel each other. But, most important for purposes of this analysis, they have all been operating to influence the external relations of the European Communities during the last ten years, and it is to the EEC that we now turn.

THE EEC IN WORLD AFFAIRS 1958–1970

In his familiar essay on the 'Possibilities and Limits of a European Communities Foreign Policy', Ralf Dahrendorf likened the EEC in external affairs to a 'fettered giant'. 'Great power and capability are there', the Commissioner wrote, 'but his hands remain tied.'[16] The metaphor is accurate, as far as it goes, but it hardly captures the panorama of EEC external relations between 1958 and 1970. Though fettered to be sure, institutionally and otherwise, the Community nonetheless has acted in world affairs, and paradoxically, despite its fetters it has acted deliberately and consistently.

The EEC has suffered, and continues to suffer, from all of the problems discussed earlier under the headings 'inappropriate central institutions' and 'missing central leadership'. Herein lie the giant's fetters. Foreign policy-making for the EEC has been part and parcel of the same laborious, time-consuming, log-rolling, horse-trading, lowest-common-denominator process by which almost all Common Market decisions are reached. In matters of external relations, as in most other matters, the Commission proposes and the Council of Ministers disposes, and between proposition and disposition lie countless committees, endless compromises, interminable delays and often years of time. This institutional tragi-comedy is recorded in such episodes as the twelve years it took to negotiate a trade agreement with Israel, the delays in the negotiations for British entry as the Six sat behind closed doors trying to decide what to tell the Commission to tell the British, and the court proceedings between the Commission and the Council over which was to represent the EEC in European road transport negotiations.

Clearly, the EEC has no foreign policy procedure as such. Neither has it a set of authoritative central roles in the field of external relations. There is no responsible EEC foreign minister, not even an authoritative committee at the Community level. Instead, there is a

[16] Ralf Dahrendorf, 'Possibilities and Limits of a European Communities Foreign Policy', *World Today*, April, 1971, p. 152.

group of national officials – the Council – who must move before the EEC can act. Consequently, there is no central leadership in the EEC external affairs sector, no elite to preside over, harmonize, and if necessary suppress, national, regional, and factional interests, no one charged with mapping an EEC course in world affairs. Rather, there are competing sub-elites, national and otherwise, who sometimes pay lip-service to European interests, but more often fight to protect pet parochialisms. To be sure, the Commission, Commissioners, and their staffs could be thought of as a central elite for the Communities. But, in terms of the actual policy process in the EEC, the Commission must be more realistically thought of as one factional interest among many.[17] Also, one is sometimes led to question whether Commission interests and European interests are always one and the same. When all of this is said, in the light of earlier analysis we might expect a pattern of 'passivity, drift and fragmentation' in the Communities' external relations. Indeed, there is considerable evidence of this in the tediousness of initiative and response, already alluded to, in the avoidance of unitary stances in UNCTAD, on monetary questions and on most issues that are not strictly economic issues, and in separate national meanderings in relations with the East.[18] Furthermore, we might also expect these institutional and leadership problems to produce internal crises at times when external pressures demand collective action from a Community that is not prepared for it. Such crises the EEC has had in relative abundance – over French Africa during the negotiation of the Rome Treaty, over the European Free Trade Area, over British entry, and over responses to international monetary problems.[19]

Yet, despite the institutional and leadership problem, there has not been as much passivity, drift, and fragmentation in EEC external relations as might have been expected. On the one hand, there has actually been a good deal of external action. The EEC has negotiated economic agreements of various sorts with more than fifty-eight states.[20] It has participated as a unit in two major rounds of multi-

[17] Glenda Rosenthal, 'Decision-Making in the European Communities', unpublished doctoral dissertation, Columbia University, 1973, Chaps. III & IV.

[18] F. A. R. Alting von Geusau, *Beyond European Community*, A. W. Sijthoff, Leyden, 1969, p. 152.

[19] Stanley Henig, *External Relations of the European Community*, Chatham House & P.E.P., European Series, No. 19, 1971, pp. 25–6; Miriam Camps, *The Free Trade Area Negotiations*, PEP Occasional Paper, No. 2, April, 1959; Nora Beloff, *The General Says No!*, Penguin Books, London, 1963, *passim*.

[20] Dahrendorf, *op. cit.*, p. 150.

lateral trade negotiations and in several UNCTAD convocations.[21]
In addition, the Communities have established a common external
tariff (CET), and a special international agricultural regime, and
they have enlarged themselves by negotiating the entry of three new
members.[22]

But even more analytically revealing than the Communities'
external activities as such has been the consistency with which
various kinds of issues and problems have been handled. There has
been, in fact, enough consistency in external output from the Communities to suggest a foreign policy, or at least a set of principles
guiding relations with third countries. For example, one detects in
Community behaviour what might be termed a principle of *non-
dilution* which proscribes external dealings that might threaten the
international identity and integrity of the Communities. This is
reflected in a certain wariness about Community participation in
more broadly based multilateral schemes such as a European-wide
free trade area, and it is symbolized in insistence upon preserving
the CET.[23] Then, there is the principle of *association*, slowly elaborated over time, which invites specialized, preferential linkages
between the EEC and carefully categorized non-members.[24] There
is too a principle of *liberalization* which sanctions bargaining aimed at
the reciprocal removal of economic barriers in the interest of expanding world trade (as long as this does not conflict with non-
dilution as discussed above or the agricultural regime as discussed
below). Concerning agriculture, one could say that the EEC has
been guided by the principle of the *sanctity of the Common Agricultural
Policy*, which forbids any external tampering that might upset
internal tightrope walking.[25] Furthermore, there is the principle of
accommodation with the United States which recognizes transatlantic
interdependence, but instructs the EEC to seek relations with the
US which more closely reflect the changing realities of the global

[21] Henig, *op. cit.*, pp. 41–5; Werner Feld, *The European Common Market and the
World*, Prentice-Hall, Englewood Cliffs, N.J., 1967, pp. 105 ff.; Rosenthal, *op. cit.*,
Chap. III.

[22] Uwe Kitzinger, *Diplomacy and Persuasion*, Thames & Hudson, London,
1973, *passim*.

[23] Alting von Geusau, *op. cit.*, p. 107, Henig, *op. cit.*, pp. 26–7.

[24] Henig, *op. cit.*, pp. 25–71; Rosenthal, *op. cit.*, Chap. III; John Pinder, 'The
Enlarged Community and the Less Developed Countries', paper presented at the
Annual Conference of the University Association for Contemporary European
Studies, 3–5 January, 1973.

[25] Harald B. Malmgren, 'Coming Trade Wars?' *Foreign Policy*, No. 1, Winter,
1970, pp. 120–1.

balance of economic power. In a negative way, a principle of *hands-off* has been operating with regard to EEC relations with state trading countries to the East. Implicit here has been the recognition that each EEC country has very good and very important political reasons for conducting its own *Ostpolitik*. Finally, until very recently, aspects of EEC external relations had been based upon a principle of *Anglo-Saxon exclusion*. This last of course is now defunct.

Hence, there have quite clearly been systematic influences operative in EEC external relations, and these have not by and large come from a central leadership or central roles. Actually what we have witnessed in the EEC during the past several years is an example of the rather classic phenomenon: a sub-elite has captured the power base of a newly integrated unit and used it for its own purposes. There is no question but that the principles underlying EEC external behaviour, as well as much of the behaviour itself, closely reflected the thrusts and directions of French foreign policy during the 1960s. While it would be an exaggeration to say that the French government controlled EEC external relations in all aspects, it is nonetheless accurate to point out that France exercised pre-eminent influence.[26] This was partly because other member states contented themselves with protecting their special interests in EEC external relations and refused to conceive of Community foreign policy as anything more than this. It was also partly because the de Gaulle government intimidated the Commission into reneging any leadership it might have exercised. Partly, too, the institutional mess in the EEC invited usurpation. But, most important, the French most subtly, and most skilfully clothed their policies in 'European' garb and convinced their partners that what was good for France was good for Europe. De Gaulle wanted French pre-eminence in Europe and a European role in world affairs, all embellished with the recognition, prestige and voice of a super-power. He also wanted revised relations with the United States which reflected new European power, independent relations with the East, freed from Soviet-American enmeshment, and a French sphere of influence in the third world. The EEC was to be one instrument, an economic one, to be used in

[26] Henig, *op. cit.*, pp. 32–3, Rosenthal, *op. cit.*, Chap. IV; Gordon M. Adams, 'Political Integration in Europe: The African Association of the European Economic Community', unpublished doctoral dissertation, Columbia University, 1971, Chap. III & *passim*. In addition, materials presented in this section on French influence were gathered during personal interviews in Brussels during 1971, 1972 and 1973.

the pursuit of these French ends. Thus, throughout the 1960s the French government saw to it that the external initiatives and responses of the European Communities complemented Gaullist goals, while the influence of other Common Market partners was felt mainly in the protection of special interests and in the modification of some of de Gaulle's more pugnacious pursuits.

But despite the appearance of deviousness and manipulation in the French attempt to capture the EEC power base, there is actually little cause for judging harshly the external behaviour of the EEC during the 1960s. To an extent, what was good for France was clearly good for Europe too. General de Gaulle's ambition and French political skills lent consistency and direction to EEC external behaviour, where otherwise there might have been a good deal more passivity and drift and some erratic bounding about. In external eyes, the EEC under French leadership acquired an international identity and some appearance of purpose. Most important, during the 1960s the external behaviour of the European Communities was by and large adaptive. The thrust of economic relations with other industrialized countries was to increase co-operatively total wealth and well-being rather than to redistribute competitively existing endowments.[27] Then, too, while the EEC was no more generous or altruistic in dealings with the less developed world than were the industrialized countries generally, substantial quantities of aid did in fact flow from Europe 'southwards'.[28]

Fortunately, too, for the EEC and the world, the international system (or at least the international economic system) was sufficiently accommodating during the 1960s to absorb any disruptive outputs the EEC might have initiated. The external aspects of the Common Agricultural Policy were among these, as were programmes of discrimination against Asian manufacturers, the announcement of generalized preferences, and the blows to Britain. Rumbling followed such actions, but the fact remains that the international system did not rain down massive retaliation upon Brussels, whereas in other days and ages and in less accommodating international systems this would have been the predictable response.[29]

[27] Dahrendorf, *op. cit.*, and Dahrendorf in *The Times*, 1 January 1973; though Krause, *The Common Market and the United States*, and Henig, *op. cit.*, p. 40, dispute this somewhat.

[28] R. Lawrence, 'Primary Products, Preferences, and Economic Welfare: the EEC and Africa', in P. Robson, ed., *International Economic Integration*, Penguin Books, Middlesex, 1971, pp. 362–84.

[29] Cf. Smith, *op. cit.*, pp. 160–2 ff.; J. H. Clapham, *The Economic Development of*

Finally, during most of the decade 1960–1970 neither the French nor the Commission, nor the elites of other Common Market countries suffered from great anxieties about rank-disequilibrium or relative deprivation in the international system, at least as far as their customs union was concerned. Few looked upon the EEC, as such, as a new 'super-power'. Rather, most viewed the European Economic Community as a uni-dimensional international actor – an economic unit solely – and questions about its appropriate political role, and the kind of status which was its due, were seldom seriously asked. In fact, such questions were blunted because of the great uncertainty about whether Europe would ever become anything more than an economic unit. Gaullist France was certainly anxious about rank-disequilibrium in the international system; but the French were concerned about France, not the EEC, which was but an instrument for them. Thus, the prompting to adventurism, revisionism and muscle-flexing which has traditionally followed from perceptions of rank-disequilibrium was largely absent in the EEC. So too was adventurous behaviour.

As they always do by hindsight, the independent variables of this analysis – institutions, leadership, elite aspirations, elite perceptions of status and international environment – rather nicely describe and explain the EEC's external behaviour during its first decade of operations. By this analysis, the Community turns out to have been a 'fettered giant', and also a 'captured giant', but on the whole it was a rather 'benevolent giant'.

SOME UNCERTAINTIES AHEAD

The future, however, raises questions about the continuing consistency and adaptiveness of EEC external behaviour, because, in terms of the elements deemed important in explaining the behaviour of newly integrated units, a number of things seem to be changing in crucial ways. First, French predominance in EEC external relations is ebbing for many reasons, including the fact that neither other member-states nor the Commission are prepared to allow themselves to be intimidated by the French to the extent that they were during the 1960s. In addition, Great Britain is now a member of the Common Market and the British appear rather intent upon injecting themselves directly and forcefully into questions of EEC external relations. Meanwhile, as French direction is weakening, the effectiveness of the Communities' central institutions, and the authority of the central elite (i.e. the Commission and related *ad hoc* groups) do not appear to be growing stronger. In the light of patterns and relationships discussed earlier, these developments could well augur a lapse into erratic behaviour as one sub-elite and then another steps in to seize control over the Communities' foreign relations. Or the result could be inconsistent behaviour as each sub-elite concerns itself with only those aspects of EEC external relations that involve its own particular, special interests. Alternatively, all this could mean passivity to the point of stagnation as sub-elites find that they cannot impose their control over a system that is institutionally unsuited to anyone trying to impose control. If this latter should become the case, we might suppose that member states will increasingly come to prefer to go their own ways in external affairs.

Let us for the moment, however, set aside this 'drift, stagnation and fragmentation' argument. It is already well known and it drives always towards the same conclusion: if the EEC does not arrive at some institutional restructuring and some reallocation of authority, or create some surrogate for these in the realm of external relations, it will not become a more effective international actor. But suppose the Communities do overcome these problems (as they well might through a system of continuous inter-governmental consultation and consensus-building)? Or, suppose that a new national sub-elite or international coalition of sub-elites (Gaullists community-wide perhaps?) gains pre-eminent influence in the foreign affairs realm? How then is the Europe of the 1970s likely to behave in international relations?

First, if we believe even a part of the rhetoric engaged in by European statesmen today, we must receive the distinct impression that goals and aspirations of both national and EEC elites are changing. This is partly because expectations are changing – a politically united Europe in the 1980s is honestly expected and many of the uncertainties about whether Europe is ever going to be anything more than an economic unit have been dissipated. Thus, the quest for a new 'European role in world affairs', a role appropriate to the new European self-image of imminent political unity, is presently capturing the pens of speech writers, the serious attention

of scholars, and the imagination of EEC populations.[30] This 'quest',
which was supported with enthusiasm at the October 1972 Summit
of the Nine, is a relatively recent development (everywhere save
perhaps in France). While the preferred nature of this 'European
role' is not yet clear, it is surely to be both political and economic
and the principles that will found it will include *equality* and *alternative*. Europe must attain equality with other great powers, and it must
be accorded recognition for this new status. Moreover, it must present an alternative to the ends, means and styles of the other powers.
Europe is to be a haven for smaller nations who seek escape from
entanglement in super-power rivalries, and Europe is to be an
object of emulation for those who wish to learn how to co-operate
regionally.[31] More cynically, all of this might be interpreted to mean
that some in Europe today rather fancy a 'European' piece of the
world, 'an almost coherent regional bloc from the Arctic Circle to the
Northern frontier of South Africa . . .'[32] In any event, the passive
stances on major world issues, the denial and shirking of political
role, the acceptance of bipolarity, the Atlanticism, and the under-
aggressiveness of the European Communities in all but strictly
economic matters, seem to be becoming postures of the past as
more statesmen today articulate, and more Europeans applaud, 'the
Community coming to take its full place as a major power in the
world'.[33]

Interlaced with this altering, and much more politically charged,
goal structure, and to a certain extent producing it, is a growing
sense of rank-disequilibrium among European elites, a sense that
others are not showing due respect for Europe's new power. For
example, Commissioner Dahrendorf, in his report presented upon
stepping down from the EEC's Directorate General 1 in January

[30] Dahrendorf, *op. cit., passim.*, Francois Duchêne, 'Europe's Role in World
Peace', in *Europe Tomorrow*, Richard Mayne, ed., Chatham House, London, 1972,
pp. 35 ff.; Commission des Communautés Européennes, Direction Générale de
la Presse et de l'Information, *Les Européens et l'unification de l'Europe*, EEC,
Brussels, June, 1972, p. 204, 'Une majorité pour l'Europe "troisième force"'.

[31] Dahrendorf, *op. cit.*; Duchêne, *op. cit.*

[32] Dahrendorf, *op. cit.*, p. 150.

[33] Speech by the Prime Minister, Edward Heath, as reported in *The Times*,
Friday, 20 October 1972, p. 6. The Prime Minister went on to say, 'so far, the
external policies of the Community have been directed towards promoting
common economic objectives by joint action. That will no doubt continue to be
their primary emphasis, though as I have implied, we must ensure that we weigh
the political with the economic as we develop the Community's external
relations.'

1973, alluded to a 'neurotic' attitude within some EEC departments –
i.e. a feeling that the EEC was being unduly criticized, discriminated
against and attacked by other major industrial countries, most
notably the United States.[34] In addition, among European political
leaders today one hears that the EEC must exert political influence
commensurate with its economic influence, an anxiety which is
expressed in the formula 'economic giant, political dwarf'.[35] At
present we see Europe (i.e. the Nine essentially) negotiating towards
an East-West security conference, 'so as not to be left out' of global
affairs, and we see Europe again preparing for disarmament talks
concerning force reductions (MBFR) so as not to be 'out-SALTED'
by the Americans and Russians. Apprehensions about Soviet-
American condominium, justified or not, are much more manifestly
a part of European elite thinking today than they were in the 1960s.
To the extent that this syndrome of sentiments about rank-disequilibrium is a new departure among European elites, and if history is
any guide, it could well be a departure in the direction of assertiveness, adventurousness, or more generally speaking, disruptiveness.

Finally, the international environment surrounding the European
Communities is no longer as accommodating as it was during the
1960s, at least where economic matters are concerned. More
specifically, the United States seems no longer willing to accept
economic penalties in the interest of European unity, or even the
myths of such penalties, nor does Washington seem predisposed to
accept much European political or economic pressure as long as
military dependence remains a fact.[36] At the same time, economic
difficulties between the EEC and Japan also appear to be mounting.
In effect, the climate of international relations among industrialized
countries of the West has become rather inhospitable, and recent
negotiations intended to solve international economic problems
have reflected growing obduracy. The frequently voiced argument
that there are reasonable men in all the industrialized countries who
are seeking amicable and mutually rewarding solutions to world
economic problems, tends to be countered by the reality that there
are also unreasonable men in all these countries who tend to wield a
good deal of political influence. Then, too, beneath these arguments
and counter-arguments lie the facts of modern welfare statism,
the force of modern public opinion, consequent inward pre-

[34] Dahrendorf, as reported in *The Times*, Thursday, 11 January 1973, p. 6.
[35] Cf. note 33.
[36] *The Times*, 21 February 1973, 'US Affirms Need for Security-Trade Link'.

occupations and external disregards, and a forecast of parochialism, competitiveness and mercantilism in international political economy set in an atmosphere of nastiness and intolerance.[37] In sum, if EEC elites are about to try to usher their new unit to higher rank and greater influence in world affairs, other actors in the international system are now a good deal less predisposed than before to move aside and let this happen. If the international game is becoming more competitive, the EEC may well become more competitive in order to play it well.

CONCLUSION

Perhaps expectedly, my answer to the question, 'how is the European Economic Community behaving in world affairs?' is that the EEC is behaving very much as newly integrated units have always behaved in world affairs. To the extent that these units have been institutionally weak and lacking in leadership, they have behaved passively and erratically; to the extent that they were able to find leadership and direction, they have acted with vigour. Most have aspired to great power status, and, when such aspirations met with frustration, pugnaciousness was often the result. Most of this is well reflected in the behaviour of the EEC during the 1960s, and, to the degree that this analysis has validity, even more of it can reasonably be expected in the decade ahead.

Finding these similarities between historical experience and EEC behaviour might be a bit distressing, especially to those accustomed to think about European integration as a model of international co-operation and a promise for peace. The fact of the matter is that, historically speaking, there is almost an inverse relationship between international integration and peace. While it is totally misleading to think about the EEC becoming involved in military contests with rivals as other newly integrated units did in the past, continuing and exacerbating economic and political conflicts involving the EEC are distinct possibilities.

Traditionally speaking, the evolution from international debut *via* integration to major power status passes through several phases. An initial period of international meekness is followed after a time by a period of growing self-awareness and realization of power and potential. This is often followed by an upwards revision of goals and

[37] Gunnar Myrdal, *Beyond the Welfare State*, Duckworth, London, 1960, *passim*.

aspirations. Then comes a period of assertiveness directed towards the attainment of higher rank and influence in the international system, which is followed by world systemic adjustment (peaceful or otherwise), followed finally by a new equilibrium and the newly emerged power's constructive participation in world affairs. In this panoramic sense, if the European Communities are not faltering for lack of structure and leadership, they may presently be entering into the beginnings of the 'assertive' phase along the way to ultimate constructive participation in an adjusted international system. If this is true, then one must conclude that the relationship between international integration and peace in this EEC case is going to depend upon all the five factors identified in this study, but most crucially upon the quality and authority of European leadership in coming years, and upon the tolerance and far-sightedness of other elites in the international system.

Karl Deutsch

Between Sovereignty and Integration: Conclusion

LET US ASK FIRST OF ALL A SIMPLE QUESTION – 'WHY DOES ANYBODY want integration?' There are usually two reasons. The first is: in order not to be killed by somebody with whom we fail to integrate. This argument for integration has been stressed by popular writers, such as Emery Reeves and others. It is a variation of the old German proverb which goes, loosely translated, 'If thou wilt not my brother be, I'll smash thy skull most certainly.' This notion that groups that do not integrate must destroy each other is a widespread but false belief. Luckily it is not true. The Scandinavians did not form any United States of the North, and yet they have not killed each other for a long time even though their ancestors were formidable warriors.

The second and more serious point is that an integrated political community can mobilize much larger capabilities, not only for one or two purposes (which could also be achieved by an alliance or by functional agencies), but for a wide range of different potential goals. In other words, integration – and more particularly political amalgamation – aims at the creation of a wide range of *general purpose* capabilities, often exceeding by an order of magnitude or more the capabilities of the component states. By integration we can put together gross national products not merely of one or two or five billion dollars, but gross national products of a hundred or even of a thousand billion dollars as in the case of the United States, and even in today's dollars that is a great deal of capability.

THE SOCIAL FABRIC OF INTEGRATION

If there are needs that require very large capabilities and a very large range of purposes of needs not easily predicted, then there is a very strong premium on political amalgamation, that is, on the creation of common governmental institutions. If the most salient need is only for peace among neighbours, then it may suffice to stick to the general ideas of safety engineering and traffic engineering. One then can have smaller sovereign states that learn to communicate sufficiently quickly, and to respond sufficiently quickly, to one another's messages, so as to avoid collisions. In the first case, in order to haul quickly a very great amount of freight we need a freight train. But if we have to move less freight over a rougher road, we may be better off with a convoy, but if the convoy is to keep together, the drivers will have to be mindful of each other's signals. In this case I think we come close to pluralism, or to what Herbert Spiro and others have called interdependence.

Integration, even of the pluralistic kind, requires a very high degree of integration of the social fabric. Communication theory will tell us that without having much in common in memories, mutual signals will not be understood. The only way to have communication between two organizations, systems or countries, is not only their possession of adequate complementary communication channels, but also their possession of adequate memories and decoding routines, so that they understand each other. In this sense, social fabrics, the social system, the social and political cultures are to a large extent the devices which serve societies for communication channels, for decoding, and for memory interpretation.

We cannot simply think of interdependence in terms of mutual bargaining or of mutual advantage. In this sense the economic model for interdependence, the model based on Adam Smith's old idea of the division of labour, is inadequate for the political problems we are facing now. Today there is something more involved. If interdependence involves the creation of common capabilities, the development of a common social fabric, the development of high capabilities for communication and responsiveness, then it can be pluralistic. If, however, we get mainly interdependence in the sense that actor A cannot act without help from actor B, and vice versa, but the social fabric is missing, the communicative capabilities are missing and responsiveness is missing, then interdependence is an excellent engine for manufacturing frustration.

There was an American film shown some years ago showing two convicts escaping, one white, one black, from a penitentiary. They got out. But unfortunately found themselves shackled together and became very frustrated indeed. It was a very instructive film – it preached tolerance but as I remember the story ended with at least one of the convicts dead. That is to say interdependence without enough communication, without enough common fabric, without enough – forgive me the horrible word – cybernetic capabilities, capabilities for communication and self steering, or, as some of our French and Belgian colleagues might say, for *concertation* – concertation of laws, administrative practices and political decisions – may be a good way for building such a fabric. However, when we begin to do market research for concertation, we soon must ask: where do the *capabilities for concertation* come from? Interdependence without concertation, without common social fabric makes social systems ungovernable, but it takes at least a minimum of common social fabric to make political, legal, and administrative concertation practicable. Size alone will not accomplish it. Aristotle once said one should never build a ship so big that it could not obey the rudder.

THE PENTAGON OF GOVERNMENTS

What Herbert Spiro has called the 'global pentagon' of the five biggest powers – and I shudder to think how this word will sound in the mouth of an angry Latin American nationalist – may have to deal with the problem of Aristotle's ship. How manageable is such a global pentagon of governments? Can it steer itself? Do its governments, elites, legislatures, and electorates have enough in common to co-ordinate the actions of the five interdependent powers? There will have to be a good deal of research, and I think in Professor Spiro's present agency and others a good deal of practical work will develop ways in which these five interdependent big powers will at least be able to govern the interdependent complex of their affairs. The answer will not be Robert Dahl's competitive pluralism written large on the international scale. Dependable co-ordination cannot be built by deterrence and bargaining alone. A world of deterrent powers, a world of bargaining powers will, as a total system, be ungovernable. There will be no invisible hand to keep the system together or to move it anywhere.

The global pentagon that is now proposed is, and I would agree, a very sensible and realistic short-term solution to buy us a little time. But it is not viable in the long run. It would become a pentagon of wealth. For the five powers pictured on the excellent diagram in Professor Spiro's paper – the United States, the European Common

Market (if it is a single power), the Soviet Union, China, and Japan – have more than half of the world's income but less than half of the world's people. It is a club – the only poor country involved is China, and it is relatively clear that the Chinese influence on what actually is done in this pentagon is relatively minor. One can make use of being nice to China to put pressure on the Russians but beyond that at the moment at least one does not see any very great positive co-operation or mutual support in regard to many common positive goals. The other four proposed partners also are not very close together, although it is to be hoped that they will become closer and that common positive efforts will improve. In Professor Donald Puchala's paper, however, we have been told that the international economic system is becoming somewhat more unpleasant, somewhat tougher, somewhat more competitive. We hear about common European measures to exclude Asian competition, meaning Japan, Hong Kong, Singapore and other places. We find that European bargaining with America is getting a bit tougher. We find that Europeans refuse to buy some of the dollars which we have refused to stop printing until quite recently. Thus we get in many ways national courses of action that create larger international problems. These are not insoluble problems but they are problems which are formidable, which will not be solved quickly, and which will not go away.

In recent years, many of us have been tempted to burn incense before the shrine of multinational corporations. But as political scientists we should not overlook the fact that multinational corporations are among the world's worst instruments for government. This has been true from the Hudson Bay Company that angered the American colonists in the 18th century to the East India Company that governed India in the 19th century, and to the United Fruit Company in our time – the company that has not succeeded in lifting some Central American republics even to an Asian level of poverty.[1] The multinational corporations do many things well but they do a spectacularly bad job in assisting or promoting good government, and they themselves are singularly poor instruments of government. One of the important ideas of President de Gaulle was that the

[1] In terms of per capita gross national product in 1965, the peoples of Honduras, the Dominican Republic and El Salvador were poorer than those of Malaysia, Hong Kong, Lebanon, and Mongolia, as well as poorer than those of Gabon and Ghana in Africa. For data, see C. L. Taylor and M. C. Hudson, *World Handbook of Political and Social Indicators: Second Edition*, Yale University Press, New Haven, 1972, p. 316.

political sector and political leadership in France, or in any country, cannot be replaced by the mechanisms of the market and the mechanisms of the corporation. Business corporations are not designed to do these jobs; they cannot do them well; but they can by their power weaken the governments and public institutions.

INTERDEPENDENCE OF NEEDS

There are three other problems. The world threshold of tolerable frustration is declining. First, in many parts of the world fewer people are willing to accept frustration in this life and hope for compensation in the other. This is even true of Northern Irish Catholics. It is observable that in place after place people arise against frustration with much more vehemence and fury. It seems that one cannot demonstrate to people human powers on the scale of the jet plane or the moon landing, and then expect them to accept the kind of frustrations their great grandparents accepted, in their social life, in their occupational roles, in their social status and prestige.

Secondly, our modern society is becoming much more verbal, information-oriented, and symbol-oriented. Words, symbols and information all are associated with languages; and language is becoming intrinsically much more important than ever before – in politics, in economics, and in cultural and social life.

As a third problem, we are witnessing a vast increase in destructive potential, created by modern technology and modern weapons systems. The interdependence of mutual destruction, the heavy interdependence of potential death has become much stronger, much faster, and much more immediate than the interdependence of life. This is one very real aspect of Professor Spiro's interdependence thesis. The interdependence of death in the form of strategic interdependence has grown so fast and so thoroughly, that it is already there. The interdependence in regard to economic and positive life is much much weaker; it even may have declined.

Since 1947 no sovereign country has given up its separate existence except for a few marginal cases.[2] It is true that a sovereignty is never complete or perfect, but its effects go fairly far. In 1913 world trade was 30 per cent of world income. In 1962 it was 22 per cent of

[2] Syria briefly merged with Egypt in the United Arab Republic but soon seceded again. The English and French parts of Cameroon voted in favour of a single Cameroon but they had not been fully sovereign states before.

world income; in 1968 it was 18 per cent of world income. During
the last sixty years, world income thus has been growing faster than
world trade. The foreign sectors in the world are declining.[3] We can
deceive ourselves into thinking that this is not so by starting our
statistical series only in 1950 or in 1938, that is, either beginning with
the devastation of the second world war or beginning with the great
depression of the 1930s. If we take what our fathers considered normal, the year 1913, as our baseline – or we could take the 1890s – we
find that the world has become somewhat more dissociated. A
serious discussion is now beginning as to whether up to a point a
strategy of selective dissociation might not have to be used together
with the strategy of selective integration, so as to make the age of
interdependence survivable. I think this is quite compatible with the
point of view of limited interdependence, as implied in Professor
Spiro's paper.

In the end we must think in terms of an interdependence of world
needs. This is my last point. We cannot act as if one could let the
majority of mankind starve. The interdependence of destructive
power today is limited to the first-class powers of the world. We still
can let minor wars go on in many remote parts of the world as a
privilege of the impotent, while the big powers cannot afford big
wars among each other any more. But by the end of the century there
probably will be about twenty or thirty countries with nuclear
weapons, each of which will have the capability to destroy New
York, Washington D.C., Moscow, Leningrad, Paris, or London. In

---

[3] Within each country, as well as for the world, the trade-to-GDP ratio is an
indicator of the relative proportions of the relative power base or power
potential – in terms of manpower and money – which internationally and nationally oriented interest groups, respectively, could try to mobilize in pursuit of
goals. To fulfil this rough but useful indicator function, for any particular
year, the ratio should be computed in prices of that year, or of a year as close as
possible to it, so as to indicate the relative share of contemporary economic
activities and manpower of each sector. To 'deflate' or otherwise change the figures for either trade or GDP by recalculating them in prices of, say, 1913,
in order to say that in terms of those prices the current T/GDP ratio would have
been different, is to miss the entire point of this calculation, which is to gauge the
relative *current* potential political resources of each sector. Unfortunately, this
misunderstanding of the method seems to have occurred in the article by Richard
Rosecrance and Arthur Stein, 'Interdependence: Myth or Reality?' *World Politics*,
26:1, October 1973, pp. 1-27, esp. pp. 5-7. For a discussion of the political meaning of the T/GDP indicator, see K. W. Deutsch and A. Ekstein, 'National
Industrialization and the Declining Importance of the International Sector',
World Politics, 13:2, January 1961, pp. 267-99.

some of these countries at least, governments will come to power that would prefer to go out with a bang than to see their people starve with a whimper. It would be a very unproductive and unprofitable choice, but, as Professor Spiro has said, we can no longer drive any substantial minority, or any major ethnic or social group, to desperation. By the end of the century the majority of mankind may not be too far from the brink of desperation given present dynamics of food, population, and ecology. In the short run the multilateral bargaining game of diplomacy will buy us time. But in the long run we may have to think more seriously about the words of Ambassador Edwin O. Reischauer that the real international problems of the world are different from the balance of power problems on which both statesmen and students of international politics now lavish so much attention.[4] The real problems – food, housing, health, usable land, air, and water, and a tolerable degree of personal security, welfare, education, and freedom – are the problems of the majority of mankind. These are the problems that are now becoming crucially important. If we bear them in mind, we will know what to do with the time which our diplomats now are trying to buy for us.

[4] See Edwin O. Reischauer, *Toward the 21st Century: Education for a Changing World*, New York: Knopf, 1973.

Contributors

David Apter *is Henry J. Heinz II Professor of Comparative Political and Social Development at Yale University.*

Max Beloff *is Gladstone Professor of Government and Public Administration in the University of Oxford and Fellow of All Souls College, Oxford.*

Ioan Ceterchi *is Professor in the University of Bucharest.*

David Coombes *is Professor of European Studies, in the University of Loughborough.*

Karl Deutsch *is Professor of Politics at Harvard University.*

Leon Dion *is Professor of Political Science in Laval University, Quebec.*

Geoffrey Goodwin *is Montague Burton Professor of International Relations in the University of London, at the London School of Economics and Political Science.*

Ghita Ionescu *is Professor of Government ,in the University of Manchester.*

Dennis Kavanagh *is lecturer in Government at the University of Manchester.*

Karel Pomaizl *is Professor of the Institute of Philosophy and Sociology, in the Czechoslovak Academy of Sciences.*

D. J. Puchala *is Professor of International Relations in the University of Columbia.*

Herbert J. Spiro *is currently a member of the Planning and Co-ordination Staff in the Department of State, USA.*

INDEX